D1552645

Strange

Short

Stories

By the Doctor

Walter Lewis Wilson, M.D.

SWORD of the LORD
PUBLISHERS
P.O. BOX 1099, MURFREESBORO, TN 37133

CONTENTS

INTRODUCTION

Anyone who has had the privilege to hear the late Dr. Walter L. Wilson in the pulpit is aware of how interesting is his message and how refreshing his approach to any subject.

Here are 128 fascinating pages of lessons for Christians from common, everyday things. Flies, peanuts, tails, tears, lead pencils, postage stamps, coal, taking a bath, candles, automobiles, soap, haircut, dogs, jackasses—did you ever hear of such an assortment to teach such wonderful, vivid lessons!

Dr. Wilson was a kindly Christian physician who knew how to drive home to the heart how Christians ought to live. He was also one of America's great and best-loved Bible teachers, profound in his simplicity.

This godly man was a very dear personal friend. He preached in the church of which I was pastor in Dallas. He preached with me on Bible conference programs. I visited in his home a few months before he went to Heaven. How he would greet me with an arm about my shoulder, saying, "My dear, dear Brother Rice!"

Dr. Wilson was an amazingly happy and successful personal soul winner, a charming storyteller and an anointed preacher.

Be sure that young people and lost neighbors have a chance at these wonderful stories.

Beans and other things

Do you know beans? Now don't laugh at this question for maybe you do not. Beans are very interesting things. Climbing beans, for instance, are left-handed. I am sure you did not know that you had been eating left-handed beans all your life.

One day as I sat in a country home looking out the window, I asked the farmer if he knew that the beans in his garden were left-handed. He replied, "You may be a good doctor but what you know about farming wouldn't cover a postage stamp."

"That may be so," I replied, "but if you will go out and examine those tall bean vines which I see in your garden, I believe you will see that they are all growing up the pole from left to right."

He felt sure that I was mistaken, but went out at once to prove that I was. I watched him as he went from vine to vine and noted the unusual expression on his face. Sure enough—all his vines were left-handed. One of my friends unwound five or six vines and then wound them up the opposite way around their poles to see what would happen. All these vines died of a broken heart because they could not have their own way.

Atheists and agnostics and unbelieving men who occupy prominent positions in educational circles can give no explanation whatever of instinct in nature. We know that the bean does climb this way but we cannot understand it. Hops climb a pole from right to left. They are right-handed. Why do they always climb that way? What sneering professor can explain this simple fact of nature? The wise man knows that God has done it. The honest man will admit that only God could do it.

Another miracle is seen in the early life of the bean. Shortly after it is planted the gardener will go out to inspect his garden. Here and there little broken places appear in the crusty ground. The clods are being pushed up by some power from beneath. The farmer will lift one of these clods which may weigh a pound or more, and which is quite hard, only to find beneath it two beautiful, soft, green leaves, soft as velvet. On each leaf is half a bean. The bean is bringing up Father and Mother to display them to the world and to show with pride what a lovely Father and Mother it took to make such a beautiful new plant.

How can these two soft leaves push up a hard, heavy clod? These leaves are so delicate and tender that if they were laid on the table, an ordinary piece of blotting paper would crush them flat. Where do they get the power that is revealed in this phenomenon? This is one of those miracles of God that cannot be explained nor understood by men. We see that it happens, but we do not know how it happens.

God can do miracles in your life if you will only let Him. Strange and enjoyable experiences are given to those who walk with God.

Have you noticed that all watermelons which show stripes always have an even number of stripes? I have examined dozens of them in the field and in the store without ever finding a single melon with an odd number of stripes.

Oranges, grapefruit, lemons and tangerines always have an even number of segments or sections. Once in a while there may be a false septum found in a fruit but upon examining it closely you will find that it is growing within a regular segment.

Bananas have a regular formation on the stalk. The lowest row or "hand" is always an even number of bananas. The next "hand" above it has one banana less, an odd number. The next row or "hand" has one less—and so on to the top of the bunch.

When our Lord said that the harvest would be gathered "thirtyfold, sixtyfold and an hundred," He was not carelessly expressing a fact. All the increase of grains is in even numbers. The cob of corn has an even number of rows and also an even number of grains upon its surface. An even number of "silks" form the tassel on the end of the corncob. Each stalk of wheat bears an even number of grains. This is true of rye, oats and barley. I have counted the seeds on many a stalk of bluegrass and always found an even number. I am led to believe that everything that bears seed produces its seed in even numbers.

Even flowers bloom and close the bloom at regular hours of the day and night. Linnaeus, the great Swedish botanist, asserted that if he were given the right kind of soil and temperature and moisture, he could plant a variety of flowers from which he could tell the time of day or night by observing which flowers were open and which were closed.

Have you ever been impressed with the fact that flowers which bloom at night are nearly always fragrant? What a wonderful perfume fills the house when the Night-Blooming Cereus opens up her beauties to the assembled members of the family. How fragrant it is! No amount of trickery on the part of man will prevail upon this plant to open its mysterious door in the daylight. The Moonflower, "a voluntary philanthropist of fragrance," ladens the night air with the story of its loveliness and greets the neighbors for blocks around through their open windows.

The sweetest graces of the Christian life often come out of the darkest shadows in human experience.

Do you not think that God was very wise, and also kind, when He provided that cherries should grow on a tree and watermelons should grow on the ground? How would you like the order reversed? The farmer would be put to no end of trouble, as well as danger, if the watermelons grew on trees. He would have to put a fence around each tree to keep the children and also the chickens from going underneath its branches, lest they be killed by the falling of the fruit. All of this would add to

9

the expense of melons. God does everything wisely and well and we should worship Him for His goodness.

Is it not strange that the roots of a tree seem to have brains? They seem to be drawn irresistibly to water. They will run around the sides of a cistern until they find a crack and then will call all their neighbors and friends to crawl in with them and enjoy the water. They will travel along the sides of a sewer pipe, seeking an entrance. Having found the smallest opening they will crush their way through in such volume as to completely stop the flow of water, necessitating great expense for the repair.

All life comes from Jesus Christ. He created every plant and gave each its own instinct and nature. Have you let Him have your life?

What About Taking

a BATH

Most everyone takes a bath at least once a year! One would think that some folks rarely ever do. Cleanliness through bathing accompanies Christianity. It is a well-known fact that the heathen are very dirty, both about their persons and their habitations. When Christ comes in, the dirt goes out. Those who turn to God through Jesus Christ desire to be as clean as possible both within and without.

The Bible has something to say about bathing. Let us refer again to that very old writer and read in Job 9:30,31 Job's soliloquy: "If I wash myself with snow water, and make my hands never so clean; yet shalt thou plunge me in the ditch, and mine own clothes shall abhor me."

Job knew the value of soft water for cleansing purposes. Job knew also that no amount of washing the outside would cleanse the inside. Bathing in snow water would be fine for the skin but would not help the soul. "What can wash away my sins? Nothing but the blood of Jesus."

Quite a strange bath is described in John 13:10. Jesus said to Simon Peter, "He that is washed needeth not save to wash his feet, but is clean every whit." We know of course that this could not be true in the physical life. Certainly washing the feet of the little boy will not remove the high water markings on his

11

neck. Our Lord was not speaking of physical things; He was referring to the walk.

How difficult it is to get children to understand that every part must be washed, and washed—with soap. Did you never smell your boy's face and hands to see whether he had washed with soap?

Just as the entire body must be washed if it is to be all clean, so the entire soul and spirit, mind and heart must be washed in the blood of the Lamb, if we would be clean "every whit."

A futile and useless bath is indicated in Jeremiah 2:22, "Though thou wash thee with nitre, and take thee much soap, yet thine iniquity is marked before me, saith the Lord God."

The person who thus washed himself with alcohol and with soap indicated that he knew that he needed a bath. He must have been examining himself and found the soiled places which needed cleansing. He sought out the two cleansing agents, which he thought would be the best. He applied them to his own self. He sought by his own efforts to remove the dirt and stains from his skin. It was of no avail.

Even though we may blot from our memory the sins of the past, still they remain inscribed on the records of Heaven. Only the living God can remove those incriminating reports and cleanse the page of its dark record of your sins.

A transforming bath changed completely the life of a great general. Naaman was the commander-in-chief of the armies of Syria. He was an honorable man, and a great man and had been used by the Lord to deliver Syria from her enemies. In spite of his wonderful position, power and noble character, he was a leper. Only God can cure leprosy. Leprosy is a type of sin. Leprosy mutilates the body and separates the leper from society.

Sin does everything that leprosy did. Naaman went to Elisha, the prophet of Israel, for cleansing. The prophet's instructions were to bathe seven times in the River Jordan. This was to prove whether Naaman was a real believer. He dipped himself in the water seven times, as he was told, and received the gift of new life, as he was promised. You will never come to Jesus

Christ for cleansing unless you believe that He can do it, and that He will do it.

Have you trusted Him and plunged into that fountain open for sin and uncleanness?

The great King David prayed once that he might have a bath that would bring peace to his heart and comfort to his soul. This prayer is recorded in Psalm 51:7: "Purge me with hyssop, and I shall be clean; wash me, and I shall be whiter than snow." This was a personal prayer: he prayed about his own need. This was a specific prayer: he prayed for a definite blessing. This was a prayer of confidence: he knew that the kind of bath that God would give him would effectually cleanse him from his iniquity and sins.

The Lord heard his petition, washed his soul and sent him out into his daily life with a happy heart and a song of praise upon his lips.

This bath which makes whiter than snow is available to all who will come to Jesus Christ and trust wholly in Him.

There was a special provision made in the Jewish tabernacle for bathing. Even though the worshiper had been to the brazen altar and had seen there the sacrificial lamb dying for him and for his sins, still it was necessary that he should go from the altar to the laver for the bathing in its waters. Without the bath it was not possible for the worshiper to enter into the Holy Place. At the brazen altar his inner soul was cleansed, but at the brazen laver his outer soil was removed.

This same procedure is true of the soul. The blood of Christ puts the sins away and washes the heart whiter than snow. The living water of the living Word cleanses the outward walk and way of the believer. The brazen altar is typical of Calvary. The laver is typical of the Word of God.

Paul has written in the book of Ephesians concerning Christ and the church, "That he might sanctify and cleanse it [the church] with the washing of the water by the word." As we learn from the Scriptures the things that are wrong in our lives, we receive grace from God to remove them from our lives. Thus we become more and more like our Lord Jesus. There is a

13

consecration bath mentioned in Exodus 29:4. Here we find Aaron and his sons being bathed as they enter the priesthood. This was a public confession that they had washed out of their lives the ways of the world and the paths in which other men walked, that they might walk only with God and might serve Him only. They removed out of their lives, by this act of bathing, all selfish ambitions, all plans for personal advancement, all schemes for personal gains. These men were to be separated men. After this bath these men were to keep themselves unspotted from the world and occupied wholly with the Lord.

The Lord enables each Christian to take the same path and to walk thus wholly separated to the Lord.

The law of Moses provided a special bath for every kind of leper, whether he be poor or rich, whether he be prominent or obscure, whether he be aged or young.

God just had one way of cleansing for every kind of leper. He must first be brought to the priest for diagnosis (Lev. 14:2). After this a sacrifice must be offered and the blood must be shed for the afflicted man (Lev. 14:5). Following this he must bathe himself in water (vs. 8).

So it is today. You must come to Christ Jesus for the diagnosis; you must accept by faith His precious blood for cleansing; you must believe His Word implicitly, fully and completely.

ANTS
Go to Picnics

The great King Solomon on two occasions has called our attention to the little ant that we might profit thereby. In Proverbs 6:6 he wrote, "Go to the ant, thou sluggard; consider her ways, and be wise." Later on in the same book he wrote, "The ants are a people not strong, yet they prepare their meat in the summer" (Prov. 30:25). Since this wise and good king has recommended that we go to school to the ant, let us do so for a while. I am sure it will be delightfully interesting.

Someone has said that the ant is the busiest creature in the world but she has time to attend every picnic. Have you not noticed how quickly the ants find the food? Not only do they hunt up every picnic but they seem to seek out every pantry. They like jelly and jam. They rejoice in sugar and syrup and are not easily kept from entering. They are most assiduous and arduous in all their labors. They are diligent and vigilant in seeking out their food. They seem to be tireless in their labors. They "work while 'tis day," and stay home at nights as all good children should do.

I took Solomon's admonition quite seriously one day and so journeyed out to the Park with the family for a picnic, taking along a magnifying glass. After sufficient search, I found a tiny path through the grass which had been made by the ants. Lying down beside the path I waited for Mrs. Ant to appear. You see, all the ants that go to picnics are females. It is a case of "let the women do the work." The male ants remain down in the ground, taking care of the babies and doing the housework. Of course, Solomon never had to do it—he had plenty of helpers.

15

I did not have long to wait until a lovely little lady ant came ambling along the path, seeking her supper. I quickly placed a chunk of bread down at the edge of the path and my little visitor soon found it. Taking as much as she could carry, she started back along the path going home with her precious burden. Another ant soon met her and I was delighted to observe what followed the meeting. The first ant laid down her piece of bread and with her front feet she gently touched the body of the second ant imparting to her in some way the good news about the location of her great "find." To my astonishment, the second ant made no effort to seize the piece of bread which the first ant had deposited on the ground. As ant number two loaded up with bread and started back along the trail, I watched both of them. Each time the performance was repeated and each time the bit of bread on the ground was unmolested.

What a lesson this is to our hearts. Chickens, or dogs, or pigs, will quickly grasp any bit of food laid down by another, and will run off with it. The ant knows no such impudence. She respects the rights of others. She admits the propriety of ownership. They disclaim all selfishness.

As the ants journeyed home bearing the precious burden, they told so many about their "find" that soon a stream of ants was on the journey, and before long all the piece of bread was stored safely away in their ground homes for the winter.

So God's good Gospel has spread. One comes to the Bread of Life and feeds to the full, then goes on his journey to tell others he meets of the wonderful treasure he has found. By tongue and by pen the news is spread that Christ Jesus is the Bread of Life. So thousands upon thousands have come to Him and others are coming only to find that the half was never told.

Each ant has four pairs of ears (some boys think their aunt has sixteen pairs of ears). There is one pair of ears in the two front legs; another pair in the abdomen; another pair in the thorax and another pair in the head. God has graciously gifted this little insect with unusual hearing ability because it is so small that it cannot see much and therefore cannot avoid danger.

God shows His care for ants as well as for elephants. He cares for you, too, no matter how small or weak or insignificant you may think you are. He cares for every moment of your life, and He wants all of your devotion and trust.

The ants are very diligent and active in the summertime because they know that the winter is coming when there will be no picnics. They dare not venture out when snow and ice are on the ground. They know better than to leave their homes when the temperature is below freezing. They have learned from some source that frozen food cannot be carried nor broken loose from the ground.

Where did the ants learn all of these needful things? Did some atheist or infidel somewhere, sometime, establish a school for teaching ants about the future? Will any of these learned gentlemen kindly step forward and tell us how the ant became so wise? Perhaps, when the ant and the elephant and the alligator and the dog all parted company from the original protoplasm, they divided up among themselves the different ways of living and were self-instructed. Who knows?

Let us gather together some of the professors from some of our great universities and have them expound this mystery. "God hath made foolish the wisdom of this world." All the law-makers, the joke-makers, the sports-writers, the money-makers, together with all the teachers and professors, with all the politicians and unbelieving preachers in the country put together could neither give life to a dead ant nor teach a live ant how to live. We have a living God on the throne who knows all about it. He can do it, and He does do it.

Moses was commended of God because he believed in future judgment and prepared for it. He knew that the avenging angel would pass through the land at midnight and would destroy all the firstborn who were not under the blood. He knew that even his own house would not be exempt. As great as he was, and as good as he was, he knew that his house must be protected by the blood. He obeyed God, he shed the blood of the lamb, he applied the blood over the door, and his house was saved.

Noah, too, was commended because he believed that there

was coming judgment and wrath and prepared for it. He did as the ants do. He prepared for trouble ahead. He built an ark. He obeyed God's Word and entered in as he was instructed. He had learned the lesson which the ants teach. Life insurance prepares for future death. Storm cellars prepare for future cyclones. Coal is bought in the summer for the cold that is coming in the winter. Christ Jesus is a refuge for the coming storm of God's wrath.

Let me urge each reader to be wise like the ant. Prepare now for the storm that is coming after a while.

We Learn From the AUTOMOBILE

We shall compare the automobile to the Christian in the story that follows. The auto is not self-made. It did not just happen. It is not a product of nature. It does not grow on trees. It was made by an intelligent man thinking out all the multitude of problems connected with its strength and its service.

So the Christian is not a self-made product. The Holy Spirit convinced him of his wreck and ruin, his need of a new birth, and Christ Jesus transformed him by the saving power of His Word and His blood.

The automobile is made for service. It is not an ornament. It is not used for show purposes. It is not merely an advertisement for man's skill and wisdom. It has a definite duty to perform and it does it well.

Even so the Christian has been transformed by the power of God that he may be of service in the harvest fields of earth and for the glory of his Master. Christians, too, have a duty to perform and many of them do it well. They carry the message of salvation to the lost, solace to the sorrowing and bear the burdens of the bereaved.

The automobile cannot guide itself. It must have an intelligent hand on the wheel. The one who guides it must not be under the influence of any evil spirits found in bottles. He must not be asleep. He must not be a lunatic. He must be sober, sane and sensible if the car is to be guided safely.

The Christian, too, must be guided. He cannot direct his own steps nor lay out his own path. "As many as are led by the Spirit of God, they are the sons of God" (Rom. 8:14). When the Spirit is at the wheel, the duty will be well done and the road will be safely traversed. Have you taken your hands from the wheel and turned your life over to the Spirit of God?

The car may be beautifully painted, splendidly upholstered, equipped with new tires, have the license plates in place—but still make no progress. There is no gasoline in the tank. It cannot go without power.

So our blessed Lord told His disciples, "Tarry ye in the city of Jerusalem, until ye be endued with power from on high" (Luke 24:49). Many of the Lord's people are trying to operate without power. They are really saved. They are clear on the Gospel. They are lovers of the Lord Jesus, but they are strangers to that blessed Spirit of Christ who alone can endue with power and endow for service. Their Christian activity is a drag, a push and a pull. They are weary in the Lord's work. They feel that it is an uphill job with little prospects of success.

Oh that God's people would take time to go to the "filling station"—that Throne of Grace—and give the Holy Spirit an opportunity in their lives.

Even though the tank may be filled with gasoline, still the car may not operate, the engine may not turn over because the battery is "down."

There are those among His people who are clear on the doctrine of the Holy Spirit. They can quote the Scriptures about His Person and work, but somehow or other there is no power in their lives. They have the theory but do not see the theory operating in their own experience.

The battery may be likened to that indescribable and yet indispensable touch of the Holy Spirit upon the soul which builds a fire under the boiler, makes "live steam" and causes the machine to throb with power. In the case of our story it is the making of the spark with the sparkplug which ignites the gas and explodes with power in the cylinder.

Have you had any explosions in your experience? Do you know the blessing of this limitless power of God manifested in the working of the Holy Spirit? Christianity is a "going concern." You will never go as you should until the power is there.

An automobile would not be safe if it had plenty of power but no brakes. Not only does it need power to go but it needs power to stop as well.

The Christian must not run riot on any subject. He must not go "to seed" on any truth. He must not become lopsided on any teaching. There must be power to restrain as well as power to constrain, in every Christian's equipment. "Thus far shalt thou go and no farther" must be applied in the everyday life of the believer. Bands are just as necessary as joints.

Gasoline is necessary in the tank but oil is necessary throughout the car. The car would soon burn itself out if there were no oil in the engine. The inward parts of the car, the clutch, the differential, must be lubricated. The outer parts of the car, the wheels, the fan, the steering apparatus must all be greased if the car is to run properly.

The oil is another figure of the Holy Spirit. Not only does He empower for service but He also equips the Christian for happy service, sweetly and kindly given. He makes things run smoothly when there is danger of friction. He makes it possible to operate with heavy loads and with great burdens without the engine heating up and sticking tight. How wonderfully blessed the Holy Spirit is in all His ministry for the Christian!

There must be cushions in the car for comfort. Who wants to ride on a hard, board seat? Comfort in the seat is a prime requisite for happy automobile driving.

Our Lord calls Himself the God of all comfort. He not only would have us as soldiers serving Him in the battlefield, but He would have us comfortable, enjoy sweet peace of the heart and the comfort of the Holy Spirit in our souls. In one place He said, "Be of good comfort" (Matt. 9:22). Our service will be more effective and our ministry more profitable if our hearts are comfortable.

No manufacturer would produce a car with no lights. Driving through the night requires sufficient light. There are dangers to be avoided. There are cars to be passed. There are curves to be negotiated. The light reveals all these dangers and enables the autoist to travel safely through the dark.

We Christians are traveling through a dark scene. The Sun of Righteousness was nailed to the cross. The shadows of sin have fallen athwart the pathways of men. We need a light to guide us safely through the maze and mist. This light is the Lord Jesus Christ, the Light of the world. Be sure that in all your arrangements for life you do not miss the Light, the Lord Jesus Christ.

Gasoline in the rear end of the car is no substitute for water in the front end. There must be a cooling system, else the engine would not operate.

Let the Living Water flow freely through your soul, that you may operate well for the Lord.

Whose tears?

The chemist would say that tears are a combination of sodium chloride, phosphate of lime, mucus and water. The pastor would say that tears are the bleeding of a broken heart. The police officer would say that tears are a sign of weakness.

There is much about tears in the Bible. Our Saviour only left two things on earth that were a part of Himself—His tears and His blood. His tears revealed that His heart was touched with the feeling of our infirmities and that He is glad to bear our griefs and carry our sorrows. His blood bears testimony to His great desire to cleanse us from iniquity and sin. In Gethsemane the Saviour prayed with strong crying and tears.

A queen's tears are mentioned in Esther 8:3. Here this lovely Jewess presented her petition to the king for the preservation of her people. The prayer was effective, the king was moved, the petition was granted. She made request for her people at the risk of her own life. These tears revealed her earnestness, her devotion, her purpose of heart.

Praying with tears is usually effective.

A farmer's tears are referred to in Psalm 126:5,6. Salt water seems to make seed grow. Why should a sower be weeping? What is there about the seed or the soil or the service to bring tears to the eyes? This passage says, "They that sow in tears shall reap in joy." The passage is referring to the sowing of the seed of the Gospel, not corn or wheat or barley.

The tears come because of the tragedy of a life in which there is no Christ. When God's long-suffering ends, the sinner's long-suffering begins. The tears are there because of the danger that lies ahead in the path of that one who has not yet received the good seed into his heart. The tears show that we believe. The tears are proof that we care when we go out with the Gospel. The Lord enable us to mourn for lost men!

A father's tears are brought before us in Mark 9:24. What a scene of sorrow this is. It is re-enacted over and over again in many homes.

Here is a wicked boy with a praying father. What anguish that father had seen as the wicked spirit had afflicted the lad. The father's heart yearning over the boy could not be comforted.

How cruel the Devil is! He wrecks the life and laughs at the wreck. He ruins the soul and rejoices over the ruin. He breaks the heart and pours liquid fire into the wound. There is no grace in the Devil's program. There is no mercy in Satan's plan.

The father's prayer is recorded in this passage as he came to Jesus and said WITH TEARS, "Lord, I believe; help thou mine unbelief." Such tears are precious in the sight of the Lord. Such tears tell of a true heart, a believing heart, a downright earnest heart. Such tears have power with God.

Bring your boy, father; bring your daughter. He will see your tears and answer your cry.

A sinner's tears move our hearts as we read Luke 7:38. Here a sinful woman is seen kneeling at Jesus' feet. She washed His feet with her tears and wiped them with the hairs of her head. Probably she had been standing in some dark doorway on a street of Capernaum when Jesus uttered that memorable cry, "Come unto me, all ye that labor and are heavy laden, and I will give you rest" (Matt. 11:28). All the men she had ever met came to rob her. They had probably taken all she had, even her virtue. They had added to her troubles and increased her sorrows.

Here was a Man who would give rest to her troubled heart.

24

She brought her alabaster box—the oriental girl's hope chest—and crushed it at the feet of the One to whom she would give her heart and her love. Christ saw those tears. They revealed her true repentance. They brought from His heart forgiveness and peace.

Have you been to the Saviour's feet with your tears? Have you ever really come to Him for what only He can give? Kneel there today, a suppliant for His mercy.

The tears of a king as he wept upon his bed in the presence of death (II Kings 20:5) remind us that even royalty may be wretched. Kings and queens do have tears, so do statesmen and bankers, admirals and presidents. The wealthy, the strong, the prominent, all have tears. Sorrow is universal. No means by men can prevent its entrance into any heart.

The tears of Hezekiah, the king, touched the heart of God and brought to him fifteen additional years for his life. Praying with tears is usually effective. Dry-eyed prayers often come from dry hearts. Dry hearts do not produce the flowers that bloom with Heaven's graces.

Let us pray the Lord to give us soft hearts.

Hannah prayed with tears (I Sam. 1:10). Here was a woman who saw the great need of Israel and prayed for a son who might bring the people back to God. She was a barren woman. Though she was barren of children, her heart was rich in its desires toward God. She saw the need of the people, she realized the need of God's presence, she craved being the instrument through whom the deliverer might come.

Again the Lord saw those precious tears, looked into that praying heart and granted the desire of her soul. Oh that we, too, might thus weep over the need and receive the answer from Heaven.

A mighty preacher had tears (Acts 20:19). The Apostle Paul who was mighty in word and deed had a tender heart. He wept over the people of God night and day. His were not dry sermons. They were moistened with tears. His were not cold sermons. Hot tears from a warm heart told of his deep love for those to

25

whom he ministered in Ephesus. He wept because he cared. These new converts were a burden on his soul. His protracted meeting was three years long (Acts 20:31). We do not know when he took up the collection, but we do know when he wept. What a model preacher he was!

May God give us tender hearts, moistened eyes and spirits that love those to whom we minister.

DOGS Stay Dogs

It is quite evident that the hypothesis of evolution does not apply in the dog family. Way back in Exodus 11:7 dogs are mentioned, and they are again referred to clear down to the end of time in Revelation 22:15. They are mentioned frequently throughout the Scriptures and never in a commendable way. It is true that the dogs licked the sores of Lazarus, but only a dog would do it. It seems strange that this pet which is so admired and esteemed among men should not find some commendable place in the Scriptures.

We all admire those wonderful St. Bernard dogs that are trained to save life in the mountain passes. We love to watch the beautiful posture of the bird dog as it "points" or "sets" before the prey. We admire the swiftness of the greyhound and the courage of the mastiff; but dogs get no word of commendation from the Lord.

"Without are dogs" is the terse comment with regard to the final ending of these peculiarly attractive animals (Rev. 22:15). Why should such a comment be found in Holy Writ? Perhaps it is because men and women spend so much time and money and affections on that which God utterly rejects. Many a one has time for a dog who has no time for God. Have you noticed that "dog" is the backward way of spelling "God"? Those who will not walk with God are glad to walk with a dog. Those who care little for God's glory, often care much for a dog's comfort. Some who give nothing to God will spend much on their dog.

God tells us that the dogs will be shut out from Heaven, and those who preferred the dog to God, will be shut out with their pets.

The price of a dog was not acceptable in the service of the Tabernacle (Deut. 23:18). The Tabernacle was holy, while the dog was unholy. The Tabernacle was clean, while the dog was unclean. The Tabernacle was for the priests, not for puppies. The time spent in the Tabernacle was profitable, while time spent on dogs was wasted. God arranged for the fellowship of saints in the Tabernacle. There was no provision there for fellowship with dogs. The presence or the price of a dog had no place in the sacred courts of God.

Our Lord Jesus compared His enemies to dogs in Psalm 22:16, saying, "For dogs have compassed me." There were wild dogs in those days. They were like wolves. They wandered around the cities seeking the dead bodies, killing and destroying and were feared by men.

The howling multitude around Calvary behaved like dogs. They shouted their epithets at Christ. They gnashed upon Him with their teeth. They struck Him with their fists. They spit upon Him. They would have torn Him limb from limb if possible.

Even today, men in hatred call each other dogs—a name of shame. Christ hugged no dogs to His bosom. He did not spend His morning in the park giving a dog its morning exercise. He held no Pekingese against His cheek in loving embrace. Christ chose the company of those who loved His Father, who worshiped God and who followed Him.

A certain class of preachers is described in the Scripture—as dogs, in Isaiah 56:10 and 11. They seek to feed themselves on the fat of the land, but give no warning to lost sinners. They love their own comforts, but have no care for the souls of the lost. They talk in their sleep, as the marginal reading gives it. They are not awake to the danger of sinners, nor to the fearfulness of the wrath of God. They are sleeping while the battle between the Saviour and Satan rages. They do not warn the wicked of his danger but accept the gifts of the wicked as the price of their silence.

These are compared to greedy dogs. They are never satisfied with anything. They are not found resting in the love of Christ. Nor are they satisfied with the Scriptures. These must give book reviews, written by others, as blind as themselves, because in their drowsiness they see little beauty in the Word of God. These do not understand the need of God's people, nor the hunger of the saints of the Lord for living bread. These look for their own gain from their own quarter and live lives pleasing to themselves. God calls them dogs, and God says the dogs will be outside the city walls of the New Jerusalem.

Gentiles were compared to dogs in Mark 7:27 and 28. A Gentile woman pleaded with Christ for her daughter. She was a believing mother. She was a praying mother. She was a mother who came to Christ about her girl. How blessed it would be if every mother did so!

Sometimes, the mother herself needs to be prayed for, because she has become the prey of the world and of Satan. Christ's answer to her prayer was, "It is not meet to take the children's bread to cast it unto the dogs." Jesus had to come to Israel, to the Jews, not the Samaritans. The humble heart of this mother at once took the place given to her and she replied, "Yes, Lord: yet the dogs under the table eat of the children's crumbs." Such faith and trust moved the heart of the lovely Lord and He granted her the desire of her heart, the healing of her daughter.

It is not easy to take the place of a dog but she did it. It is humbling to be called a dog, but she was willing to be humble. It would be considered an insult by some if they were called dogs, but she accepted His diagnosis of her case and took the place which He gave her. This is faith. This is victorious faith. This is conquering faith. This faith gave her back her daughter.

On the gates to many farm houses may be seen the sign, "Beware of Dogs." This is really a Scripture found in Philippians 3:2. There Paul wrote, and the Holy Spirit has preserved the statement through the centuries, "Beware of

29

dogs." Certainly he was not referring to the animals of the street. His warning was against cruel men, misleading men, selfish men, men who invite the gift of your confidence and trust, and then bite the hand that held it out. These are false, religious teachers. These are ungodly men who teach and preach a gospel which is not of God, and a faith which is not from Heaven.

Beware of everyone who denies the deity of Christ, salvation by grace alone through the precious blood, the complete inspiration of the Scriptures, the eternal conscious punishing of lost sinners, and the physical resurrection and return of the Lord Jesus Christ. Dogs eat their own vomit, but saints feed on the Bread of Life.

The Hen Egg

Among the many wonders in nature, eggs hold a top place. The mystery of the hatching of an egg cannot be explained by any of the great minds of the world. Eggs hatch in multiples of seven days. The eggs of the potato bug hatch in seven days, those of the canary bird in fourteen days. Hen eggs hatch in twenty-one days and duck eggs in twenty-eight days. One species of the mallard hatches her eggs in thirty-five days. The eggs of the parrot hatch in forty-two days.

Things do not happen by chance in nature. God ordains all the affairs of life—whether it be in the animal kingdom or in the vegetable kingdom.

Have you considered how it is that the beautiful feathers of the peacock on which are accurate markings should be brought forth out of an egg which contains only yellow yolk and colorless albumen? How did the colors get there? Why are the colors always those that belong to that particular fowl? How is the figure formed on the feathers in such a way that when the tail is spread the markings are perfectly in place and beautiful in appearance? Only a living God can do this. But to refer again to the hen egg, let us proceed.

The shell on the small end of the egg is much thicker than on the large end. The baby will emerge from the shell through the large end, therefore God has arranged and designed the shell so that the baby can easily peck its way through where the shell is thin.

At the large end of the egg there is an air chamber. This may be seen when the shell is removed from the hard-boiled egg. When the baby chick is formed in the egg, it is so placed that its head is in the big end of the egg and its little bill is in the air chamber. No matter how much the mother hen may turn the egg over and over during the three weeks of the hatching period, she never disturbs the position of that baby. This is another miracle of God. Man could not arrange it so, and neither can we understand how God does it. No matter how many times the egg has been turned or played with by the child, spinning it on a plate, the contents of the egg are not disturbed. The baby will always be formed with its nose in the air chamber at the large end.

The formation of the yoke should be observed. It is built like a battleship. The lower part of the yolk is rather dense and heavy, while the upper part is light and thin. This causes the yolk to float upright at all times. In addition to this, there is a rope of albumen which is attached to the two sides of the yolk, and on the other end is attached in a mysterious way to the inside of the shell. This attachment is a very slippery joint, so slippery, in fact, that no amount of spinning the egg will cause the yolk to turn over. These ropes hold it upright. It is because of these ropes that the cook must, with her finger, scrape out this part of the "white" of the egg.

The little bill of the baby chick is so soft that it cannot peck its way through the hard shell. For that reason God makes a special tool which is to be used only once. This is in the form of a tiny cone, made of a very hard substance, which exactly fits over the bill of the baby. It is with this hard cone that it breaks through the shell. There is just enough air in the air chamber to last the little thing two days. As the baby starts to breathe and the hours go by, there comes the time when the last breath of air is taken. The air causes the little one to swell up somewhat and as the chick lunges forward to get another breath of air which is not there, the impact forces a hole through the shell, and the swelling of the body cracks the shell sufficiently so the chick can emerge. Within about two days after it is born, the hard cone falls from its nose. It is of no further use. Sometimes the cone sticks to the bill and the farmer must pick it off with his fingers. How kind God is to little chickens!

Is it not strange that these baby chickens know their mother? They never had seen her before and maybe the eggs from which they were hatched came from many miles away, laid by a different hen in a different state. What forms the bond of attachment between a baby chicken and the mother hen who hatched it? We do not know. No one knows. It is another of the wonderful mysteries of God.

Have you ever asked the question, "Why does the chicken not fall off the roost at night when it goes to sleep?" You couldn't sleep on a stick, or on a fence or even on a very narrow shelf or ledge. This brings us to another beautiful example of God's skill and wisdom. The tendons from the four toes of the chicken form a single tendon in the ball of the foot. This tendon then winds round on to the front of the leg, passing through two deep grooves, thence up to the thigh where it spreads out into a fan-shaped muscle. While the leg is extended, the toes are spread open so the chicken can walk. When the chicken sits down, however, this tendon is put on a stretch across the joints and draws the toes shut. As long as the hen sits down on the roost, her toes automatically and tightly clutch the perch and she cannot fall off even when sound asleep. You see, if God did not make provisions for the hen's sleeping safely, we would have a bunch of nervous wrecks among the old hens and the eggs would cease. How terrible that would be!

The beautiful relationship that exists between the mother hen and the babies who are hatched out from her brooding is used by our Lord to illustrate His own love and care for us. In Luke 13:34 Jesus said, "How often would I have gathered thy children together, as a HEN doth gather her brood under her wings, and ye would not."

We find that there are four times or occasions on which the mother hen calls her babies under her wings. One time is when she finds a bit of food, a crumb, or a worm, or a bug. She quickly sounds the dinner call and the babies come running for the dainty morsel. So Christ said, "He that cometh to me shall never hunger; and he that believeth on me shall never thirst" (John 6:35).

Another occasion is when the experienced old mother sees an ominous black speck in the sky which circles round and round getting larger all the while. She now utters a very excited cry and calls the babies together from the menacing hawk. On another occasion she hears the thunder, sees the lightning flash, feels the cold wind blowing the leaves. Quickly she clucks her call of danger and calls the babies to shelter from the impending storm. Now at last as the shadows fall and the sun is set, she quietly calls her little treasures to sleep and rest.

Oh, that you might come to Him too!

The Noble

Jackass

The ass is no mean animal. It has played an important role in the affairs of men and occupies a prominent place in the Holy Scriptures. It was an ass which received the great honor of carrying Jesus into Jerusalem when He should have been crowned King. This was certainly a Royal Ass and perhaps was also a redeemed ass. In Exodus 13:13 we read, "Every firstling of an ass thou shalt redeem with a lamb,. . . . [or else] thou shalt break his neck." This ass was allowed to live, therefore if it was a first-born, a lamb had died to save its life. Now the redeemed ass was to carry on his back the Lamb of God who was to die for lost men.

God had ordained that the lamb must die for the ass and God has also ordained that "the Lamb of God" must die for man who is born "a wild ass's colt" (Job 11:12). Have you been redeemed by the Lamb? Only those whom He has redeemed will have the joy of living with the Redeemer. It is God's eternal decree that "without the shedding of blood there is no remission." Have you never said, "What an ass I made of myself"? If you didn't, it was just the natural qualities of the ass exhibiting themselves. We are each one like the ass, and we must each one be redeemed by the blood of Christ.

When Jacob would bless his twelve sons, he said of one of them, "Issachar is a strong ass couching down between two

35

burdens: And he saw that rest was good, and the land that it was pleasant; and bowed his shoulder to bear, and became a servant unto tribute" (Gen. 49:14,15).

What an honor was thus conferred upon this young man; he was a burden-bearer. He had two burdens: one was the burden of the people. He was willing to bear these loads that others might find rest and enjoy the pleasant land which God provides for those who walk with Him.

We read in Galatians 6:2, "Bear ye one another's burdens, and so fulfil the law of Christ." This was to be Issachar's work in life. Do we bear the burdens of others, or do we add to their burdens?

There is a very celebrated ass which is mentioned in Numbers 22:28. This was not a gentleman, however, but a lady. The passage reads, "And the Lord opened the mouth of the ass, and SHE said unto Balaam." God gave this ass, which was a female, the voice of a man. Peter writes, "The dumb ass speaking with man's voice forbad the madness of the prophet" (II Pet. 2:16). Peter must have known what he was talking about when he called this lady ass "a dumb ass." It is also rather strange that this lady should be speaking with a man's voice. Why did she not speak with a woman's voice? No wonder the prophet was frightened. He heard a dumb ass begin to talk intelligently and he heard a lady ass talking with a man's voice. This was enough to impress anyone. This ass fell down under the prophet.

The ass on which Christ rode did not fall down on the job. It was a male animal. It yielded immediate submission to the Master and carried Him safely through to the end of the journey. How many of us do fall down on the job? We are set free that we may carry the Lord here and there, but how often we fail. Let us seek grace to prove true to the end.

Balaam's ass did not talk like an ass. She spoke the words of God. She spoke the truth in kindness. She did not waste any words. She did not talk back nor waste time in palavering. She did not find fault with her master, nor complain of her lot. She got right to the point and finished when she got through.

What a lesson this is for all the messengers of God, whether

36

ladies or gentlemen! The few words this ass did speak were worth recording and saving through the centuries. The Lord enable us to heed the message which says, "Let your speech be alway with grace, seasoned with salt" (Col. 4:6).

It is quite significant that Saul, the first King of Israel, lost the asses which he should have kept. David never lost the sheep; he kept them. The relation between these two men and their animals was a picture of the relation which they would afterward bear to the people over which they were to rule. Both asses and sheep need to be kept. Both of these animals are prone to stray. The human heart also loves to wander. Bypaths are better than the highways in the opinion of the ordinary human heart. Stolen waters are sweeter in the opinion of many than the waters out of their own cistern. Saul's boyhood days were connected with asses which are a type of the lost sinner. David's boyhood days were connected with sheep which are a type of the believer.

Asses were still asses way back in Job's day, many centuries ago. So far as we know, no animal has ever changed its form or its characteristics from the time God made them until now. I have never seen nor heard of a single bit of evidence to prove that humbug hypothesis of "evolution." I utterly reject the entire scheme and plan of the teachers of this so-called theory, and shall do so until evidence is produced which proves that there has been a transition of species.

In Job 1:14 we read, "The oxen were plowing, and the asses feeding beside them." The ox is a type of the clean Christian while the ass is a type of the unclean sinner. The oxen were busy serving their master and producing valuable work for their owner. The asses were engaged in eating up that which their owner possessed and that which the oxen produced.

How like the case of the sinner and the saint this is! The believer works for his Lord, while the unbeliever works for himself. The Christian seeks the good of his Master, while the sinner lays up treasure for himself.

In Isaiah 1:3 are these words, "The ox knoweth his owner, and the ass his master's crib." Here we find the same truth exemplified. The ox cares for the one who cares for him, while the ass only wants the grub of his owner. The ox has a devotion to his master. The ass only cares for the master's gifts. The ox seeks the fellowship of the one he serves, the ass cares nothing for the fellowship if he can have plenty of fodder.

Spiritually speaking, we find that the Christian loves Christ, while the sinner only wants Christ's gifts. The soldiers at Calvary did not want the Saviour; but they gambled for His garments. They did not want Him; but they did want what was His. Which of these groups represents you? Would you ever draw near the Lord if you had all of His gifts for which your heart craves? If your lot should be cast where the crib was large, the grain and the clover plentiful, the shelter secure, would you care for the One who gave it to you? The ox gives thanks in the restaurant for the food before him. Do you thank the good Master for what you receive?

It was a young animal and a small animal that our Lord chose for His triumphal journey into Jerusalem. Our Lord will take you, too, even though you may be young and small and even obscure. Just let your Lord have all of you and you, too, may carry Him along the path of life.

EVERY FLY GONE

EGYPT

God made a thorough job of cleaning the flies out of Egypt. We read in Exodus 8:31, "He removed the swarms of flies from Pharaoh, from his servants, and from his people; *there remained not one*." Do you believe that? Not one fly left in the whole land of Egypt? Egypt was a land of flies and still is. The flies of Egypt have ruined the eyes of Egypt. What terrible stories have been told us and what fearful pictures have been shown us of the flies around the eyes of the babies of that land. Flies are on the sores of the poor. Flies are a scourge of the country.

Just the ordinary number of flies that we have are no end of trouble. A great industry has been built up in the manufacture of flypaper, flysprays, flyswatters and flytraps. Thousands of dollars are spent yearly, and countless thousands of minutes are spent daily, fighting flies. There are houseflies and green bottleflies; there are horseflies and sandflies. Flies by any name are a miserable nuisance and a harmful pest.

When God would reveal to Pharaoh something of His power, He did so in the following manner:

"There came a grievous swarm of flies into the house of Pharaoh, and into his servants' houses, and into all the land of Egypt: the land was corrupted by reason of the swarm of flies."—Exod. 8:24.

These were not just ordinary houseflies; there were flies of every sort and kind and variety. Asaph said, "He sent divers sorts of flies among them" (Ps. 78:45). There were not just a few flies; there were millions of them. The flies were in the kitchen and in the closet; they were on the bread and in the milk; they filled the bed and the bureau; they were all over the dining room table, the parlor, and the sitting room. They covered the musical instruments and got in the dough after it was kneaded. They were in the shoes and in the sleeves of the garments. They were on the walls and on the carpet. They filled the barns and the buggies and covered the horses and the cows. The humming and the buzzing and the biting of the flies was ever present day and night.

Think of the kindness of God in preventing a pest of this kind in your house. Why is it that God does not permit the propagation of these filthy, dirty insects to such an extent now as He did in Egypt? His restraining hand shows His grace and love. His kindness is revealed in His care for us even in such a small matter as the restraining of the fly population.

When Pharaoh pleaded for mercy, Moses prayed for God's delivering hand. God answered by giving "marching" orders or "flying" orders to the flies. And did they fly! From the sitting room and the bathroom; from the bedroom and the library; from the dining room and the kitchen; from the cellar and from the sink—away they went! They left the barnyard and the barn. They left the palace and the prison. They left for good.

Now notice this wonderful statement recorded by the Holy Spirit and preserved through the centuries: "THERE REMAINED NOT ONE." EVERY fly was gone. Absolutely gone, gone bag and baggage. Gone for good.

Say, my friend, did you ever try to make one fly go anywhere, and did you succeed? Beloved, I call this a wonderful miracle which only God could perform. Only a personal God could do it. Only an omniscient God could do it, for He must know where every fly is. Only an omnipotent God could do it, for He must be able to make every kind of fly obey. AND HE DID. How wonderful it is to have this God for our God!

The fly is strangely made. It has a thousand eyes, or perhaps to be more explicit, it has a thousand facets on its two eyes. When you approach a fly with a swatter it really sees a thousand swatters coming after it. No wonder it jumps and jumps fast. A fly has approximately one thousand hollow hairs on the bottom of its six feet. When the fly places its foot down, a tiny bit of glue is forced out of these hollow hairs and causes the foot to stick to the glass or to the ceiling or wherever it is walking. It is for this reason that the fly can easily climb the windowpane or walk upside down on the ceiling. Who would have thought of such a thing but a very wise, and a wonderful, living, personal God.

The horsefly lays her eggs on the front knees of a horse. The reason she does so is because the eggs of a horsefly are hatched out in the alimentary canal of the horse. Who told this fly that the horse rarely licks its hind legs? How does this fly know that the horse very frequently licks its front knees? Where did this fly learn how to get its eggs inside the horse? The fly could never lay its eggs on the tongue of the horse. It must have been given wisdom and understanding concerning the proper place to lay them so the horse would swallow them.

Has anyone started a school for flies to teach them where to lay their eggs? Have any of our scorning infidel friends taught the flies this secret? Shame on the unbeliever. Only a personal, living God could impart such information to such an insect. Even if man knew how to do it, he certainly would never do it, for he is not in the business of raising horseflies. He is in the business of getting rid of them. God alone can give a fly a fly's nature and make it live like a fly. God alone can give you a Christian nature, the nature of the Lord Jesus Himself, and make you live like Jesus.

Why do we have flies? Why does God permit men to be tormented with them in the homes, in the office, in the barn and in the field? Why does God permit the torture which flies inflict on horses and cows? Why does God permit this pest and scourge to force us to spend fortunes in fighting it and preventing its entrance?

Houses must be screened. Barns must be sprayed. The

animals must have nets upon them. The baby must be covered with a netting. We must buy swatters. We must spend our valuable time chasing flies when we should be enriching our hearts. Wicked men are made more wicked by flies. They curse and swear at the little pest until you would think that the fly would fall dead either from fright or from the poison of those ungodly lips. The optician should be glad that there are flies. How many thousands of glasses must be replaced because in knocking the fly from the nose, the glasses were knocked to the floor and a new pair was necessary! Let us thank God that He keeps down the flies as much as He does.

"Harness the Horses"

Jeremiah 46:4

The above words were spoken by the Lord to Jeremiah and therefore are fraught with meaning which will surely be rich to our souls. Farmers and teamsters will be especially interested in some of the peculiar lessons which we may learn from a set of harness.

Let us observe first that **the harness speaks of death.** Some animal died that its skin might be taken and made up into this set of harness.

Death is essential for service. The Christian who will not die daily is usually of little service to his Lord. It is those who are dead to the world who are alive unto God and who carry out His purposes and plans.

Harness speaks of intelligence. Everyone cannot make a set of harness. The maker must understand what he is doing, must understand the different parts, must know the purpose for which it is used, must know how strong it should be, must know what size is required. All of this speaks of an intelligent mind working to produce the harness.

Again we are reminded that all the works of God tell us that there is an intelligent God, a Mind that is actively at work in contriving and devising blessings for man and beast. Only God can make leather, man cannot produce it. Only God can make an animal with a waterproof skin.

How unhappy a situation would arise if the horse should absorb the rain and drown while grazing in the pasture. The skins of animals as well as the skins of fruits and vegetables are waterproof, made so by the Lord. It it were not so, we could never take a bath, we would drown in the bathtub.

Harness speaks of service. No one purchases or even makes a set of harness just for an ornament. The harness is not hung up in the parlor for a thing of beauty and a joy to the eyes. Harness is made in order that the horse may be utilized for the blessing of man. The breast strap is there that the horse may pull; the holdback strap is there that the horse may retard the progress of the vehicle. The harness is made of a certain weight when used with the buggy but it is made much stronger when used at the plow.

It is quite so in Christian service. Our Lord enables some to do the pioneering work of the Gospel where strong men are needed, men and women of endurance, of vigor, of vision. Others are chosen to do the easier work at home; there is not so much strain, there the path is lighter, the work is more easily done, the conditions are more propitious.

The harness must have in its design a provision for comfort, else it will pinch or bind or rub and produce distress, pain and soreness. The collar must be made wide, large and soft; the girth must be made wide that it may be more comfortable; the halter must be made to fit over the ears and around the mouth without binding or injuring. The bit must be made smooth so that it may not hurt the mouth of the horse.

Our Lord has said to His people, "My yoke is easy, my burden is light." He too fits His service to the Christian in ways that are comfortable so that the servant of God may say, "The lines are fallen unto me in pleasant places" (Ps. 16:6).

The harness may also speak of beauty. It may be dressed up with brass rings or rings of bone and celluloid. Sometimes beautiful jewels of colored glass adorn the harness at prominent places. The buckles may be very fancy and larger than is really necessary just to add to the beauty. Chains of rings with attractive tassels sometimes adorn the harness of an exceptionally beautiful team. Particularly is that so when the horses are on exhibition.

All is not drab in the service of our King. He makes it most attractive for those who will permit Him to do so. The flowers and fruits of successful service are most delightful. What greater joy can there be than that of serving with profit so that hungry hearts are melted with the mercy of the Master.

Harness speaks of fitness for it must be made to fit. The Shetland pony cannot wear the same harness as that which is required by the larger draft horse. Horses are of different sizes and require harness of different sizes. The wise farmer will not put a large harness on a small horse nor a small harness on a large horse.

Saul placed upon David his huge armor, but Saul was a giant and David was a lad of small stature. The armor could not fit the little boy. It was a beautiful armor, no doubt it bore the insignia of the king; perhaps it was beautifully engraved and decorated; no doubt it was made of the best steel available or made of brass. Nothing finer or better would be found in all the land—but it did not fit. We read that "David assayed to go." Of course he could not go. The Lord never expects us to fight in the armor of another. He will provide each one of us with a harness for the battle, harness that will fit ourselves. He knows the size of our hearts and the dimensions of our heads; He knows our minds and is well acquainted with our ability. He will give each one the harness for His service which is best fitted to his needs.

By means of the harness the horse is enabled both to go and to stop. There are times when he should stand still. The harness is made so that he can do both.

It must be so in our own lives. There are times to go and times to stay; there are times to pull and there are times to hold back. If God has equipped us for His service, we shall be able to do both successfully.

It may be that **the harness has upon it** a part which is called **the kicking strap.** This is necessary because the horse is prone

45

to kick with its hind legs and the strap is so adjusted that the horse cannot raise its hips to kick.

How sad it is when we see a Christian upon whom God has to put a kicking strap! Sometimes a saint of God becomes a chronic kicker. He complains about everything in the church and out of it. He is displeased with the pulpit and the pews, the music aggravates him and the ushers annoy him. He doesn't like the hymnbooks nor the songleader; the pianist plays too loudly and the preacher talks too fast. This friend needs a kicking strap to hold him down and make him work. No horse can kick and pull at the same time. When he is kicking, he is not pulling; and when he is pulling, he is not kicking.

We have noticed that **some harness** is made with **blinders at the eyes.** These serve the purpose of preventing the horse from seeing the driver. No Christian should have blinders on his harness.

The Holy Spirit is the Driver of the believer and we should keep our eyes upon Him constantly, we should be sensitive to His will and respond immediately to His touch. We should ascertain His purpose and plans and lend ourselves readily and willingly to them.

No harness would be **complete** without **two lines.** These are for the driver; by means of these, the rest of the harness serves its best purpose. The lines enable the driver to communicate his mind and will to the horse.

In the Christian's harness, the lines represent the Old and New Testaments. They are in the hands of the Holy Spirit; by means of these He guides and directs us in the paths that please Him. Through these we learn the will of the One upon the seat of the carriage; by these we are enabled to carry out His plans, to go where He wants us to go, to stay when He wants us to stay.

May the blessed Lord of our lives, the Spirit of grace, find each of us like a willing horse, clothed with the harness of God, ready and willing to follow His gracious leadings.

TALES
ABOUT
TAILS

Some animals have tails and some do not. Some have long tails and some have short tails. Some have smooth tails and some tails are fuzzy. Frogs, toads, and guinea pigs have no tails. Why should they have tails? Flies never bother them, and they do not need tails with which to hang from the limb of a tree. God used wisdom in arranging the tail business and this tale is in order to bring to our attention some of the reasons for tails.

The tail of the dog tells a remarkable story. You can almost tell the feelings of the dog by watching his tail. Some way or another the heart is closely connected with that member. If the dog is happy, he wags his tail very rapidly. If he is scolded, his tail begins to wag slowly and more slowly, as he looks pleadingly into his master's face for mercy. "His tail between his legs" tells a sad story of defeat; he has been whipped.

On one occasion I had to whip my beautiful little puppy, Gwendolyn. She was a brown water spaniel with long ears and big web feet. Her favorite indoor sport was clawing the curtains and the drapes in the parlor. I obtained a very tiny switch and gave her a few light strokes with it to observe her actions. She crouched down on the floor, her tail moving more slowly all the time until it almost lay motionless. As I scolded her she began to crawl nearer and nearer, watching my face intently. After enough punishment I laid the switch down, smiled and spoke kindly to her. How that tail did begin to wag! Her sorrows were forgotten in the bliss of present forgiveness. The wagging of her tail told the story.

The kindness that exists between cows and also between horses is revealed in the way that they may be seen standing together in the pasture during the hot summer days. Two cows or two horses will stand close together but in opposite directions; in this way the tail of one animal keeps the flies off the neck and shoulder of the other animal. They care for the little things that bother one another. They have an interest in the welfare of each other. They promote the comfort of each other.

What a blessing it would be if we were of the same mind, and sought to add to each other's joys, and never to increase each other's burdens.

Most monkeys have long tails. They hang with them, they swing with them, they play with them, they climb with them. By means of these tails they may reach out and pull the branch close to them and so obtain the distant food. By the clever use of the tail they make a quick getaway, a safe escape from the enemy.

Moses was told by the Lord to take up the serpent by the tail. It immediately turned into a rod. I have known of mountaineers who by quick action would pick up a snake by the tail, and in a moment crack it like a whip, breaking the neck and bruising the head. The Scripture tells of Samson who captured a number of foxes, tied the tails together by two and two, fastened a firebrand to the tails, and turned the foxes loose in the standing grain of the Philistines. Whoever would have used tails with which to wreak vengeance and to inflict so much damage (Judg. 15:4)!

Just to show the details of the Bible, we read in Job 40:17 about the elephant that "he moveth his tail like a cedar." Does God notice how an animal moves its tail? Certainly He does. He made it. He devised and designed all the muscles that are used in moving that tail, and certainly is familiar with all the details of it.

Let us ever remember, and never forget, that God is interested in every detail of nature, and that the Lord Jesus created every detail of it.

Israel is sometimes compared with the head, and at other times with the tail of all the nations. In Solomon's day Israel was the head, but when Jesus was on earth, Israel was the tail. When Israel rejected Christ, her place was lost among the nations, and no more was she to rule and reign as the head until Christ should return and be received by Israel as her Lord, her King and her Saviour. Israel just now is the least of the nations, but is rapidly returning to her place in Palestine, where she will become the head of the nations in a future day.

What is more beautiful than the tail of the peacock or more delightfully interesting than the tail of the lyrebird. Only God could make such a wonderful creation. The peacock's tail is for beauty, and so are many others. The design, the blending of the colors, the wavy curls, the wonderfully soft texture, all speak of the marvelous beauty of our wonderful Lord.

The One who made these beautiful feathers is more wonderful and more beautiful than they. No human mind would ever have thought of creating so interesting an appendage on a bird. Our God delights in beauty. He desires to make each Christian beautiful in life and character. He can do it, He knows how.

I saw an unusual sight in Southern Missouri one day. A peacock and a turkey gobbler were strutting back and forth with their tails spread to fullest extent. They were seeking to outdo each other in displaying their beautiful tails. For some time they paraded back and forth, close to each other out in the barnyard. As I watched them with much amusement, I saw the peacock suddenly drop his tail-feathers and run quickly down toward the orchard to disappear among the trees. Upon making inquiry the farmer told me that the peacock had suddenly seen its own feet, which are very ugly. He was so ashamed that he

49

ran away to hide and would not return to the house for two or three days.

Perhaps we would do less strutting, and have less pride, if we too were to observe the defect in our walk and way instead of boasting ourselves over others.

Birds that do a great deal of flying, such as the eagle, the buzzard, the dove and the lark, use the tail to guide the flight. They can retard or increase their speed or can float gracefully through the air by properly spreading the tail. God designed this for them, and the God who thus cared for birds, cares for you. He would like to guide you by His grace, save you through His mercy, and give you as an eternal gift to Jesus Christ His Son. How can you expect to safely navigate this life, or traverse the stream of death, without the rich provision God has made in the gift of His Son?

TREE LEAVES

Leaves are common and yet quite uncommon. In Isaiah 64:6 are these words: "We all do fade as a leaf." In this short statement, we may learn many lessons about our lives which it will be profitable to observe just now.

Only God can make a leaf. Each leaf has life, each leaf denotes the plant or bush or tree from which it fell. Each leaf in itself tells whether it is a new leaf, young in days, or an old leaf that has withstood the storms of the season and is ready now to fall.

In this respect human beings are quite like the leaf. There are young ones with their soft tender years, their lovely trusting hearts, their sweet ways and with the buoyancy of youth. The years pass by and these begin to fade and to fail as the leaf on the tree.

Leaves are not fruit. Leaves in the Bible speak of a profession and a confession which may or may not be accompanied by fruit. Our Lord found a fig tree on which there was "nothing but leaves." He expects more than leaves in our lives. He would have us laden with fruit for His glory and blessing for our fellowmen.

Leaves are born to die. They appear in the spring and we know quite well that they shall fall in the autumn. By examining the leaf after it has fallen, we may tell something of its experiences through the summer. Some fall full-sized, unmarred, beautiful in color, glorious in tints; whereas others fall curled, shrunken, sear and yellow and even perhaps eaten by worms and other enemies. Some are split and torn by the savage winds. The condition of the leaf tells either a story of protection and progress or a story of adversity and hardship.

So it is in the life of a man or a woman who reaches the end of the long summer of life. A sudden gust of wind, some disease, or some accident may quickly tear the soul away from its moorings and it is blown to the grave. Some fall in the midst of the summer of life from the glorious heights of the tree-top to the gutter of the street, to become soiled and wrecked long before their time. Some hang on through all the storms of the seasons and cling throughout the winter to the limb of the tree as though it would not let go this life. These are they who live on, past allotted threescore year and ten, past ninety, and attain even the century mark.

Some believers grow more beautiful as they grow older. Others give a benediction of peace as one sits in their presence. Some develop most beautiful traits of character when the hair becomes whitened with the wintry blast and the face becomes wrinkled with the sorrows of the summer. Others become more cruel as age creeps on. They give way to their passionate tempers, they become unruly, hard to live with, unreasonable in their demands, unsatisfied, faultfinding and critical. These are the leaves, such as fall from the cottonwood and the peach tree. There is nothing attractive there, nothing beautiful. This leaf falls in the wind, is swept away from sight and is never missed.

Leaves, such as the hard maple, which cling through the winter season, do not drop from the tree until the new life appears in the balmy springtime. The fresh young buds push off the old, dead leaves and what the storms could not do, the new life does.

How true this is today in our social system. The older men who have served faithfully through the years are pushed out of the way and lose their positions because of the advent of younger men with their fresh courage and their buoyant ambitions. Thus the leaf must leave its accustomed place and be cast aside to wither and wilt and waste away.

There are leaves which are so beautiful in the fall of the year that the school children gather them, place them in their memory books, take them to school for the botany teacher to see, and save them for after years.

In gathering these lovely leaves, many leaves are ignored by the children because they are not attractive. They do not appeal to the child's sense of beauty or value. There are those in life who are like this. They seem to serve only themselves. They do not care to develop those Christian graces which will make them beautiful throughout their life and especially lovely in their last days.

Fig leaves proved to be only false finery for EVE. They shriveled and shrank and left her exposed to the eyes of an offended God. So today, leaves of profession will not suffice to hide the soul from the living Lord.

Haircuts and Bedsteads

Who would go to the Bible to learn about a haircut or a bedstead? Beloved, you can go to the Bible to learn many interesting things which you might think were not there. If the living Lord takes the trouble and the time and the space to record such little insignificant things, we may also be sure that there are some profitable lessons in these accounts for our hearts.

In Deuteronomy 3:11 we find the short obituary of a great king. Most of the record as described in the verse is not concerning the king at all, but is a description of the bedstead on which he slept. How would you like to have placed on your tombstone a description of your bedstead with very little about yourself? Did the Lord make an error when He wrote this biography? Did Moses write the wrong thing when he wrote about the bedstead instead of about the mighty giant who slept on it? No, there are no mistakes in the Bible.

This bedstead represented the character of Og, the king. Og was a giant. He needed a large bed. Og was heavy. He needed a strong bed. Og was restless. He needed a wide bed. Og was self-centered. He provided a bed for his own personal use. Such are the lessons we may learn from this short story. The bedstead was made of iron to make Og secure and safe from damage. He looked after his own personal security and welfare. He saw to it that no hurt would come to himself.

This bedstead was about fourteen feet long and about six feet wide. He was looking out for his comfort. He could stretch without bumping his head or jamming his toes. He could roll over without fear of falling out. He provided well for his own comfort, joy and happiness. He cared nothing for God. He persecuted God's people. He despised God's will. The bedstead was a picture of his life. Therefore, the Holy Spirit, through Moses, has selected the bedstead as the subject of a sermon on the life of Og who shut out God.

In Isaiah 28:20 we read of a bed that is too short for a man, and covers that are too narrow to wrap him sufficiently. In this Scripture the bed is used to show how utterly insufficient are all human expedients to satisfy human desires.

The God who made the heart is the only One who can satisfy the heart. You may make a bed of ease for yourself, but thorns will be found in it eventually and tears will drench it before you are finished with it.

The care that the Lord shows toward those who love the poor is illustrated by these words in Psalm 41:3, "Thou wilt make all his bed in his sickness." A better translation would be, "Thou wilt smooth out all the wrinkles in his bed when he is sick."

Does God notice wrinkles in beds and the discomfort which this little thing may cause? Yes, your loving Lord is interested in everything whether little or big when it concerns the peace, the comfort and the happiness of His child.

It is quite evident that Peter had been raised well either by his mother or by his wife. In Acts 9:34 Peter spoke to Aeneas and said, "Arise, and make thy bed." This man had been in bed eight years. It would be no easy matter to make such a bed, but one of the signs that the man was really healed would be that after rising from that bed of sickness, he would smooth out the covers, tuck in the corners and make up the bed nicely and attractively. Christians are supposed to be neat and clean as well as orderly. Do you make your bed, or leave it for the weary, worn mother to make after you have left the house?

Absalom had a haircut. The Scripture tells us about it. The record of this haircut has been preserved through the centuries.

This was not an ordinary haircut. It was the haircut of a beautiful man. Absalom was the son of David, the king. His obituary is found in II Samuel 14:25 and 26. His beauty is recorded, for in all Israel there was none quite so handsome as he. Once a year he had his hair cut because it was thick and long and needed trimming. The weight of the hair that was cut off was six and a half pounds. The Lord has even taken the trouble of recording the weight of the hair that was taken off with the shears.

You never weighed your hair, did you? Did anybody ever interview you about your haircut so it could be put in the libraries of the world? Why should God want the story of his haircut to be known by all people everywhere? It was because this short story contains such important lessons for us.

Absalom lived for the beauty of his body and the glory of his person. He had a beautiful body, the Scripture says so. He did not have a wen or a wart, a bunion, or a pimple on his entire body. His feet were as perfect as his face. His fingers were as delicate as his features. No doubt he spent many hours before the mirror and in bathhouses and with the manicure, keeping himself in beautiful, fit condition. God gives him credit for all of this. God always gives credit for anything that He can.

Absalom could grow lots of hair but he could not develop any grace in his heart. Absalom cared for the beauty of his body but neglected the development of his soul. Absalom was careful to protect his body from any harm but neglected to preserve his soul from sin. He lived a wicked life and he died a wretched death. He left all his beauty in the grave. What a warning to the rest of us!

Another haircut is described in Judges 16:19. Samson was a man of God. He was a Nazarite and under the laws of God was not permitted to cut his hair. The long hair on his head was a public indication that he had accepted the vows of the Nazarite and had given his life over to God for holy uses. The Holy Spirit had filled Samson with unusual strength. He had done mighty deeds. He had slain many men. He had carried off the gates of the city. While he walked with God, he accomplished God's purpose.

One day in an unguarded hour Samson fell in love with Delilah, a Philistine maiden. She won his confidence and turned his heart from God. Worldly sweethearts always do. The best of the Devil's children make the worst enemies of God. Samson confided to this stranger the secret of his strength.

One time while he was sleeping, she had those long locks of his hair cut off. He should not have been sleeping in her arms. He should not have been loving one who was an enemy of God. With his locks shorn, the Spirit of God departed and left him helpless in the power of his enemies.

May the Lord keep us from ever making such a fatal mistake.

THE PEANUT IS CROOKED

Why are peanuts crooked? No man made them that way—pecans are not crooked. God made peanuts the way He wanted them made, and our business is to learn what we may from this interesting little nut.

Peanuts are like folks—all of them have a crook in the life somewhere. None are entirely straight and smooth from start to finish. Everybody has something wrong in his system or his disposition. Some are very badly bent—others are fairly straight. None are absolutely perfect.

The peanut is equipped with a double covering. The outside one is the one that the public sees. It is harder and more tough than the inner one, which is a thin skin covering the nut itself. Folks do not see the inner one until the outer one is broken.

Human lives are like this. There is an outer life which the public sees when we leave the home and enter the shop or the office. The inner one is revealed in the home with the wife and the children and with God. It is of a much different type. It is not at all like the outer one. Many who are delightful in their office life are crabbed and sour and hard to live with in the home. Men who are kind and sweet to the stenographer are cruel and harmful with the sweetheart they swore to love, honor and cherish. What kind of lives do you live?

Peanuts are developed in the dark. After appearing on the

58

plant, they are covered up with soil and grow to perfection and maturity out of sight, beneath the ground.

It is so in our lives. What we are, what we learn, what we do, privately and when alone, largely determine what we shall be before the world. The Lord Jesus said, "There is no man that doeth any thing in secret, and he himself seeketh to be known openly" (John 7:4).

A very wise man once said, "Who can make that straight which he hath made crooked?" (Eccles. 7:13). All the power of political leaders, all the influence of financial leaders, all the assistance which might be rendered by leaders of education, would utterly fail to make one peanut straight. Man can make many things, but he cannot make that straight which God has made crooked. Only the living Lord could make a peanut grow smooth and straight in the ground.

We find it so among people. No amount of culture or education or refinement; no amount of money, or position, or power can make a sinful heart righteous and upright. Only the Gospel can do it—only the grace of God can bring it about. God can do it and God does do it. Thousands of men and women have been reclaimed by the Gospel, but I challenge every infidel, atheist and agnostic to produce one human life that has been changed from sinfulness to saintliness by the message which he has given.

Each peanut has a sweet heart. No matter how peculiar the shell may be, when it is broken, the heart may be reached. How good those peanuts are. The smell of them intrigues you and entices the nickels out of the pocket. You can hardly resist them. There are two nuts in each shell as a usual thing. We might say there are two hearts within that shell.

It is just so with ourselves. The Christian has a heart for God and a heart for those in need. The sinner has a heart for himself and a heart for his own interests.

We do not care much for the shell—we hardly look at it closely, we care so little about it. When we buy peanuts we wish to get at the hearts immediately. We read that the "Lord looks on the heart." He too knows the difference between the outer shell of profession and the inner substance of possession.

Because there are two nuts in the shell, we are reminded of the fact that God made man for a companion. He said, "It is not good that the man should be alone" (Gen. 2:18). Our Lord sent out His disciples by two and two. Peter had a John whom he loved. Paul had a Silas with whom he suffered. Philip found a Nathaniel to whom he would introduce the lovely Jesus. This truth seems to be confirmed by the great King Solomon when he said, "A brother is born for adversity" (Prov. 17:17).

How sweet it is to have a chum in whom you can confide and on whom you may lean in times of stress and distress. Peanuts come in pairs, within the shell.

The peanut has no value unless it is broken. How strange it is that the sweetest graces are usually seen emanating from the saddest of sorrows. The roses are crushed that the perfume may delight our hearts. Meats and vegetables must be cooked that they may have value for our bodies. The animals must die that we may have shoes for our feet. Gold is melted and beaten and shapened that it may adorn us and enhance our attractiveness. In the Jewish tabernacle everything from the front door to the back wall spoke of sorrow.

The peanut is no exception to the rule. We can only obtain the good meat of the nut by crushing the shell. Perhaps you have complained because there have been crushings in your life. Do not complain—"consider the work of God" and seek to understand what blessings you may receive from your adversity.

All peanuts are the same color on the outside. God looks down on men and gives this conclusion: "All have sinned and come short of the glory of God" (Rom. 3:23). This statement is prefaced by the short, terse message, "There is no difference!" God has concluded all men under sin that He may have mercy on all. All are dead in sins, all are guilty, all are stained with their guilt, all are alike in the respect that they are lost.

Has Christ Jesus saved you?

Some Lead PENCILS

The writer has an excellent collection of lead pencils gathered up while traveling around the country. These have a peculiar interest because of their variety and because of the many helpful lessons which we may learn from a consideration of their peculiarities.

Some of my pencils are long, reminding us of those who live long lives and write upon many hearts. Other pencils are short and continually keep before us the brevity of life and the few lives that some may touch. Some of these pencils are quite large, while containing only a very small lead in the center. Others have a very small wood body, but the lead is as large as those just mentioned. Let us consider together what we may learn from these many features.

As some pencils have large leads in their hearts, while the hearts of others are very small, so we find some folks who have large, liberal hearts and others whose hearts are small, stingy and selfish. Some of these hearts are soft and write very easily with a slight touch; other hearts are hard and write with difficulty and only after much pressure. Sometimes the writing of these hard hearts makes a scratch and a tear on a white page. Soft hearts never do this. Our Lord does not want us to have hearts of stone.

My pencils are of various colors. Red, white, brown, yellow, black are found in the collection. These represent the five great races of earth. They all have hearts; they all have some purpose

61

in life; they all write something on those whom they meet in their daily walk.

None of my pencils grew in the woods. A pencil must be made by an intelligent man. Man himself had to be made by a wonderful God who is an individual, intelligent Person knowing more than the man whom He made.

Pencils made of wood represent death. The wood was once a living tree which had to be cut down, split, torn, dressed and made into form and shape for the pencil maker. So there could be no Christian without the death of the Saviour. He gave up His life at Calvary that we might take that life and be Christians.

The pencil must have a new heart before it will write and be of service. The old heart of wood is removed and the new heart of graphite is inserted. The old heart of the sinner cannot be used in writing the story of God's grace. A new heart is given when the soul trusts the Lord Jesus Christ for his salvation.

Pencils must be sharpened if they would be of use. Not every Christian can say, "I am ready to preach the Gospel." Some sharpening is necessary. The world must be laid aside. The Holy Spirit must sit on the throne of the heart. The Word of God must fill the mind. Self must be denied. Lost souls must be won.

Should we not ask our Lord to keep us sharp and ready for His service?

In my collection I have a very large pencil which looks as though it would be a wonderful writing instrument, making a large clear mark for marking large packages, boxes, etc. This pencil is a hypocrite. It is not a pencil at all. It is shaped like a pencil and is painted to represent a pencil, showing the lead, rubber eraser and the metal band around the eraser. It is solid wood, however, and can make no mark whatever.

There are folk like that in our neighborhood. They claim to be Christians, they live nice clean lives, they are taken for Christians by those who do not examine carefully. Alas, they have the form only. They have never received a new heart from God. They have never been in the hands of the Holy Spirit to be brought to Jesus Christ. They are not what they seem to be. Are you like this?

Some pencils are automatic. The lead must be forced out. There is plenty of lead in the barrel but an intelligence must cause it to project that it may be used. That Christian who is in the hands of the Spirit of God will find himself being twisted and turned and pressed that he may write the better.

One of my pencils is very expensive. I believe that my friend paid six dollars for it. Another of my pencils cost one cent at the corner store. Which one do you think will write the better? Of course you say, they will both write the same if they are held by the same hand. Quite so. The story that is told and the writing that is made depends upon the hand and the mind of the writer.

The Christian himself is in the hands of Christ. He may take a college professor, represented by the six-dollar pencil, or the janitor of the church represented by the one-cent pencil, and write just as good a story with the one as the other. Christian scholarship is to be valued, of course. Wealth and position and power are not to be deprecated by any means. But neither one has any power unless the power of the Spirit of God rests upon that man or woman.

Two of my pencils are white. One of them is white on the outside and it has a white heart but has cedar wood between. This represents the Christian on earth. Hidden beneath his beautiful exterior are motions and desires and thoughts which hurt his heart and which he would gladly be rid of. The other pencil is white all the way through and represents the believer in Glory when God has removed every vestige of sin and its effects.

Most of my pencils bear the name of the maker. God brands His sheep with the marks of Calvary. Christians are crucified folks. They have died with Christ at the cross. "The mark of the Beast" will be the Devil's brand upon all those who do not belong to Jesus Christ and have never been born again.

Most pencils have an eraser on one end to care for the mistakes that are made by the other end. We make many mistakes in writing upon other people's hearts and lives. Only the blood of Christ can erase sin marks.

Let us always abide near the cross, loving the living Lord who hung there.

CANDLES are interesting

Candles are used all over the world, but there are no candles in Heaven. In Revelation 22:5 we are told, "They need no candle." In many churches candles are used as a part of the religious service, but the time is coming when candles will not be permitted in any church in the world.

This is distinctly affirmed in Revelation 18:23. Candlelight was the earliest artificial light spoken of in the Scriptures. In Job 18:6 Bildad said, "His candle shall be put out with him."

Very often by sages and by poets human life has been compared to the burning of a candle. How beautifully Edward Henry Bickersteth described the ebbing of his own life as he dreamed the story. "The lamp that hung suspended in my chamber slowly paled and flickered in its socket." The burning flame consumes the wax and as the taper wears down shorter and shorter we know that the end is near.

So it is in life. The flame shines brightly but the life shortens and finally the candle flickers awhile, flutters, and sputters for a moment and then the light is extinguished forever. This seems to be the thought that Bildad had in his statement.

The candle is sometimes used as a type of the testimony of the life. Job seems to use it so in his book, chapter 21, verse 17.

Oftentimes the wicked flourish. They develop great gifts for men. They shed light upon many important matters pertaining to human comforts. They invent and devise means for human blessing. They neglect the Light of life Christ Jesus; their candle burns dim and they go out in the dark.

David on the other hand uses the candle as a type of his own blessing and usefulness to men. So in Psalm 18:28 he said, "For thou wilt light my candle: the Lord my God will enlighten my darkness."

Candles are made in all sizes, shapes and colors. Strangely enough, no matter what color the candle is, the light is always the same color.

Herein we see the beautiful picture of the testimony of God's people out of every country, kindred and community. The gospel story by the black man is just the same as that which is told by the white evangelist. The Chinese preacher gives the same sweet message of grace as the Hindu convert. The red man of the plains gives the same message as his black brother across the sea. No matter what the color of the candle, it is the same beautiful light of the Gospel that shines forth.

Very large candles are made with large wicks that they may give greater light. David Brainerd was such a candle and so were Carey, Hudson Taylor, Moorehouse, Moody and Finney. God gave these men wide vision, a great grasp of His Word and a deep desire for lost souls.

Other candles are smaller. They do not give out as great a light but in their measure they give out as good a light. There are wee tiny candles which are placed upon the birthday cake. Did not our Lord say, "Out of the mouths of babes and sucklings hast thou ordained strength" (Ps. 8:2)?

It is the heart of the candle that burns. We apply the match to the wick which is the very center of the candle. Our hearts, too, must be touched before we will give out light for men.

Most education does not touch the heart. Much of our Christian training in colleges and seminaries leaves the heart cold and unmoved. It is in the heart that the flame must be kindled if other lives are to find their way to the Saviour's feet.

In shining for others, however, we shall consume ourselves.

Do you remember that there were candles in the great banquet hall where Belshazzar held his feast? The writing on the wall was against the candlesticks. God has always made sure that His message is placed where men can read it plainly. The candle is a human product. It is made by men's hands. It was designed by men's minds. It burns out with the using.

God will have no candles in Heaven because in that blessed place the light of men's minds is not needed, and the product of men's brains is excluded. All the light of Heaven is that which emanates from Himself and from the Lamb.

The candle and the broom are brought together in Luke 15:8. The candle reveals the dirt and the broom cleans it out. The candle finds the coin and with the broom she drags it out from under the radiator. The candle has no virtue except to reveal. The candle may expose the dirt, but the broom and the brush and the mop are needed to remove it. The candle may shine upon the soiled hands or face but has no power nor efficacy for the cleansing of them.

Men's schemes and plans for the betterment of the world are of this sort. Investigation committees are formed to investigate difficulty and troubles, but the evil remains. Great foundations are established and much money invested for the purpose of ferreting out the causes of crime. The causes are discovered, but humanity has no remedy for the trouble after it is exposed.

There is only one antidote and preventative and remedy for the ravages of sin—the Lord Jesus by means of His Word and His sacrifice at Calvary. The clean-up campaigns of men may be likened to the polishing of the railings on a sinking ship, or giving a brush and comb to a bald-headed man.

Christ used the candle in Matthew 5:15 as a type of Christian testimony. Salvation is not a secret. It is not a blessing which we are to hide within our bosoms, nor to cover up with our business nor to secrete in our homes. Our profession and our confession are to be the means of turning many others to Christ and leading the feet of many into the narrow path of peace.

The Lord said, "Let YOUR light so shine." YOUR light is

YOUR own. No one else can shine like YOU do. No one else can say what YOU should say. No one else can give the testimony that should come from YOUR lips.

Be sure the wick is trimmed. Be sure the chimney is clean. Be sure the candle is in a prominent place where everyone can see the light. Christ would have His child as a distinct outstanding testimony for His glory. Let us take advantage of the opportunity and shine brightly, not in a small corner, as the song says, but right out on open highways in the places of concourse.

Some candles are long and some are short. So the Lord permits some to shine just a short while, a few months or years, at best. Others are granted many years of happy, useful ministry covering a full generation. It is the Master's business what size candle He makes. The Master must apply the fire to make it burn. It is our business to keep burning until we burn out for God.

In many ways, the Christian may be likened to a fountain pen. This pen is not a natural growth; it is not found in the woods, it does not grow on plants, nor is it dug from the earth. Some intelligent being conceived the idea and then produced it in its present form.

So the Christian is not a natural product. He is born as a sinner, he loves to sin and is not naturally a Christian either in heart or in practice. God must make a Christian and He does this through the saving work of Christ Jesus and the regenerating work of the Holy Spirit.

The fountain pen is made to be used. It has a purpose in life. No one intended that it should lie about on the table or on the floor unused and with no value. It has a definite work to perform in life and is made by its maker in such a way that it will do the work intended for it.

So God has equipped the Christian with those talents and gifts which will enable him to carry out God's plan in God's way and in God's time.

The pen is subject to the will and the wish of its owner. He may cast it aside for a while or he may use it continuously day by day. The pen should never complain if it is not being always used, nor should it ever find fault with its owner because he uses it too much or too little, or at the wrong hour of the day.

The pen is committed to the will of its master without arguing and without faultfinding.

No pen will write by itself. A hand must hold it. That hand must be guided by a thinking mind. The pen produces nothing original. It only transcribes on the paper the thoughts and the desires of its owners.

So it must be with the believer. In the hand of our Lord, we shall be instruments whereby He can write on human hearts the story of His love and grace from His holy Word.

No pen can write of its own volition or desire. There must be placed within it the ink, for it is by means of the ink that the impressions of the owner are placed upon the paper. This ink represents the Holy Spirit. The believer is dipped in that gracious Spirit and writes on hearts by means of that Spirit. A dry pen will not write and neither will an unspiritual Christian. The point of the pen may be of gold, but even so it must be dipped in ink. The gold point cannot do what only the ink can do. Paul said that, "Like a pen he was writing on human hearts." He specifically mentioned that the letter was written, "not with ink, but with the Spirit of the living God" (II Cor. 3:3).

The pen must be kept well supplied with ink and frequently filled if it is to be always ready for the service of its owner. The Christian, too, must be constantly filled for the Master's use.

The story that the pen writes must be worth reading. It must be a good story worth the time of the reader. It must be a profitable message. It must be written legibly and plainly that it may be easily read by those who are in a hurry or by the uneducated. The story should begin kindly and should end graciously.

The pen should not scratch the paper on which it is writing, else a scar and a mar will remain which will bring dishonor on the fair name of this fountain pen and its owner. Such marks are not easily erased. Such damage is not easily repaired.

How careful we should be in writing on the hearts of others so that we leave a clean white sheet, not soiled with blots and splotches, not injured by scratching and tearing! The damage done in a few moments may never be repaired in years.

This pen should lend itself readily to the hand of the one who holds it. It should write heavy or light, as he may desire to press it down. It should always write as he picks it up and never be out of humor or filled with something else besides the ink. It should have such a smooth point that it would make beautiful letters and be attractive to the eye of the one who reads the story.

Some hearts, like some paper, must be written upon very carefully. Some paper is very soft and somewhat rough so that the fountain pen would need to be very cleverly handled to prevent the ink from spreading and the paper from tearing. Other paper is so glossy and highly polished that the pen may have some difficulty in making an impression that will be legible. The wise writer will know just how to use the pen as it lies in the hand of its owner, yielded and still.

May the Lord make each of us a fountain pen, filled with good ink, His Holy Spirit, and ready for the Master's use.

A Wonderful

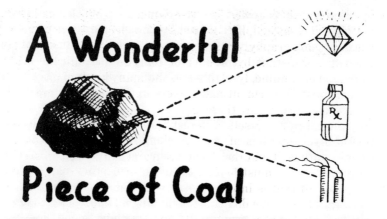

Piece of Coal

Whenever you see a pile of coal, take off your hat, bow your head and worship God for His lovingkindness. The Lord knew that we would have cold winters, so He provided the coal before we needed it. The fact that He provided it at all is unanswerable proof that He loves and cares for His creatures. He made the winters, but He provided for our comfort in the midst of winter. He hid the coal in the ground where it could not be wasted, then gave men the needed knowledge and power with which to find it and to mine it.

Think of the potential possibilities that are hidden in a piece of black coal. From it we may obtain light, so that we may turn the night into day. By means of it steam is created for operating the dynamos in our power houses, that electricity may light the nation. By it power is obtained for driving our locomotives, propelling great ships, operating machinery of every kind.

By means of coal our homes are heated, our office buildings made comfortable, our meals cooked. Coal furnishes the heat for thousands of factories. Coal makes it possible for our children to go to school in the wintertime and be made comfortable in the classrooms. Coal operates farm machinery of many kinds and propels road machinery of many descriptions.

Coal is the original source of coke, tar, ammonia, gas, graphite, and many other important and useful substances.

Indirectly from coal and its by-products we obtain pitch for roofing purposes, sulphur, Prussian blue, benzol, carbolic acid, dyes for photography, dyes for cotton, dyes for wool and silk. Aspirin is a distant by-product of coal. So are salicylic acid, cinnamon oil, aniline, lysol, phenol, and many kinds of oil.

Coal must lie dormant and useless until the magic touch of man makes use of all these potential possibilities. It has no power whatever in itself. The ordinary person cannot develop these useful qualities of coal. A chemist must do it. Not all chemists can do it, but those who are trained in coal chemistry.

Your life, too, must be in the hands of One who is able to bring out all that is in it, and the best of its possibilities. The Holy Spirit alone can do this. He knows what you are best fitted to do, and He knows how able you are to do it. Romans 12:1 is God's invitation to you who are washed in the blood of the Lamb to let the Holy Spirit use your body as He sees fit. He will make your life a success.

In order for the coal to impart its power to us, it must lose its own identity; if it is to give heat, it must be burned. If it is to impart power, it must be thrown into the furnace. If it is to radiate light, it must be set on fire. Nothing can save itself and still be a blessing to others. Even Christ laid down His life that the believer might have life. His enemies said truly, "He saved others, himself he cannot save."

By the destruction, the alteration, the conversion of coal we obtain potent medicines, beautiful colors, fragrant perfumes, active acids, powerful gases, valuable dyes, excellent water-proofing materials and ink for writing purposes.

What a miracle it is that God should take carbon, which is a black insoluble, tasteless, odorless basic principle, and by His magic touch turn it sometimes into sweet white sugar, sometimes into beautiful brilliant diamonds and sometimes into black useful coal. Only a wonder-working God could make coal, which is such a wonderful asset to man, and from which may be obtained so many useful and necessary substances.

Man with all his wisdom would never have devised a piece of coal. It never would have entered his mind that one article could have been made in the earth, from which there might be obtained 123 or more distinctly valuable materials for the daily use of men.

These products are used in the factory, in the parlors of the rich, in the palace of the king, and in the cottages of the poor. The by-products of coal are found in the drug store, the hospital, and the doctor's office. You may find them in the beauty parlor, in the restaurant, and in the laboratory. They are found on the roof of the house and on the shelves of the grocery store. Ice is made from a coal product, and the dyes in your garments are probably from the same source. We should do as the prophet said, "Declare among the people his doings."

Coal is always black wherever it is found; and men are always sinful wherever they are found. Coal is useless until man utilizes it. Sinners likewise need a divine touch from Heaven to transform their cold, hard lives into warm, useful, radiant lives to be a blessing to others.

The perfumes which we obtain from the by-products of coal are valued highly by the queen and prized greatly by the lover. Who does not delight in perfume? Even so can God bring out of the sinner's life fragrant graces of character which will bring joy to the hearts of many.

As the chemist brings from the black coal through its by-products its most beautiful colors, green, orange, yellow, red, blue, violet, mauve, brown and indigo, so the Lord can take each life that is presented to Him and bring out of it traits of character which will beautify the life of the owner and which will enable him to glorify the God of his life.

As coal contains within itself tremendous power for producing power, so the Lord picks up man, saves him, endows him with wonderful gifts and endues him with His Spirit of power. Such men go forth from the presence of the Lord to move the hearts of many. Such a man was Spurgeon; Moody likewise had power over human hearts. Luther stirred the world and the Wesleys transformed England. The potential possibilities of a saved man are wonderful. Oh, that we might let the Chief Chemist work on us to accomplish His wonderful purposes!

Some coal is called "soft coal"; another kind is "hard coal." Some kinds are termed "semi anthracite"; this kind is between hard and soft types. Hard coal may be used where soft cannot. Each kind serves its own purpose.

Is it not so among Christians? Some of God's people have very soft, tender hearts and are easily set afire for the One they love; others catch the flame slowly but may burn with heat more fierce and produce more force and power than the other.

May the Lord of Glory have the right of each life that He may make of it what He will.

Christians are NUTS

Song of Solomon 6:11

Strangely enough, our blessed Lord has recorded for us these words, "I went down into the garden of nuts to see the fruits of the valley." If our Lord compared His people to nuts, then the suggestion is worthy of our careful consideration and we shall surely find much profit in meditating on the comparisons and contrasts between the people of God and the nuts that grow so richly throughout the world.

Nuts are found everywhere in almost every climate, and in nearly every nation. So we find that Christians also may be found in every clime and among every people. They are found in greater numbers in some parts than in others, as nuts grow more profusely in some sections than in others.

Nuts grow in high places. They grow on trees and sometimes the trees are very high. So Christians are seated in heavenly places in Christ, they dwell in the heavenlies, their place is with God, they walk in the highways of life and should not be found in the swamps.

Nuts are of many colors. Some are brown, others are black, while still others are yellow. In this respect they are quite like Christians for there are brown Christians in India, and yellow Christians in Japan, and black Christians in Africa, and there are red Christians in the American desert and white Christians everywhere.

Nuts have a sweet heart. The shell covers the heart but the heart is there. All of God's people have precious hearts, most of them have tender hearts, hearts that are a blessing to others, hearts that prove useful to others, hearts that others love.

Nuts are found in clusters and in groups. One tree may have a thousand nuts upon it. Brazil nuts particularly are always found in clusters and walnuts grow in the twos and threes.

Among believers we find a fellowship also. "Where two or three are gathered together" our Lord is present. We are told to "not forsake the assembling of ourselves together." Christians love the fellowship of other Christians, believers desire to be with other believers.

Nuts are good for food and are profitable in commercial trade; they have great value. The sale of nuts reaches a very high figure everywhere in the markets of the world.

Christians too are very valuable; they are the salt of the earth, they are precious in the sight of the Lord, they are the balance-wheel of society, they are the stable element in all civilization. In the affairs of this world, Christians hold the reins, and Christian principles guide the counsels of men.

Some nuts have thin shells while those of others are thick and hard. We find it so with God's believing children. Some are easily touched, others seem cold and apparently repel the friendship of those they meet. Some are easily moved to tears while others seem hardened to the needs of men. It is easy to reach the hearts of some while others resist every attempt to reach the heart with pleas of mercy.

Nuts are like seeds—they may be planted in order to reproduce the trees on which they grew. Nuts have the power of reproduction; they really are the seed of the tree from which they fell.

Christians too should be reproductive. Every one has the power and the privilege of making known the story of redeeming love in such a way that others will believe and be brought into life, light and liberty. That Christian who does not reproduce himself in others surely has failed of God's plan and neglected the opportunity given by his Lord.

77

Nuts are durable—they stand the storms, they are not easily injured by adverse conditions. They are constantly exposed to the elements, but the elements only make them rich with nutrition, sweet and tasty for their owner.

So the believer is exposed to the elements of life. Storms of adversity may whip him around, gales of trouble may buffet him sorely, but he still keeps his place on the blessed tree of life and flourishes under the storms to which he is subject.

Only God can make a nut. The great cocoanut or the little filbert alike are the products of God's hand. No human being can make a pecan, a walnut or a chestnut. A nut is a miracle; no one can understand how the substance of the nut can come through the little stem that holds it to the tree. No one knows how the tree can draw from the soil certain elements and transform them into the nut.

Christians also are a mystery. Only God can make a Christian, the power of the Holy Spirit working in the human soul transforms that individual into a Christian, a believer in Jesus Christ, a child of God. How He does it no one knows; the fact that He does do it, every one knows.

Nuts must be broken to be of value. In the breaking the heart is revealed; the nut loses itself that it may be a blessing to others. God's children find this to be true. Only as we too are broken will the precious ointment of the heart flow out to refresh and bless others. He who saves himself cannot save others. He who saves his own life, said our Lord, will lose it.

Christ Jesus gave life to us by laying down His own life. The nut must be taken from the tree, it must be crushed that the shell may give up the lovely treasure which it holds within its bosom. In breaking and giving we, too, may have the joy of bringing happiness to the hearts of the hungry.

Some nuts appear unattractive to the eye. There seems to be nothing there that would please those who have them. They are rather forbidding in their appearance. The color is not always attractive, the shape is not always interesting. If we know, however, that there is a nut-meat, then we shall break the shell to find the meat and the meat is always there.

There may be those Christians who appear to be rough and heartless and cold. In those very hearts, however, may often be found the sweetest fragrance of Christ and the most tender care for others. Let us not judge by the outward appearance but rather let us judge by the heart which is inside.

Most nuts are gathered in the autumn. After the blighting frost, after the cold of winter has touched the trees, after the leaves begin to fall and the shadows lengthen, then the owner gathers in the nuts.

This is the ordinary way of life. God gathers His own usually in the autumn time. The hair has been touched by the snows of many winters, the shadows have lengthened across the pathway of life, the world has lost its beauty for the heart and mind, then the Lord takes Home the nut with the precious heart. The nut that has stood so many winters, endured so many storms, but was found upon the tree until the Master plucked it for Himself.

The sweet heart of the nut is surrounded by three coverings. There is the outer husk such as the walnut wears; after this, is the hard shell of the nut. This may be smooth as with the pecan or fairly rough as with the English walnut or it may be very rough as the American black walnut. The third covering is thin and is found inside the hard shell and enclosing the actual meat of the nut. This skin is most noticeable in the almond.

These three coverings represent three positions occupied by the Christian. He, too, is surrounded with three coverings. The first is the characteristics which the world sees, the second is those traits of character which his most intimate relatives, such as the wife, the mother, the daughter, see. The third is that life which only the Father sees and the Holy Spirit and the Lord Jesus. This is the hidden life—unknown to man but naked and open before God.

May our blessed Lord grant that everyone who reads this message may have a deep desire to become one of God's nuts, bring joy to the Lord and blessing to men.

OLD SHOES
and
others

There is a romance about shoes which one would hardly think of as he sits in a shoe-shining parlor observing the strange variety of shoes being polished. Shoes may tell a story of sorrow and of tears as the bereaved mother takes out of the drawer those baby shoes; the little one who wore them has been laid away. The shoes are kept to remind the broken heart of the sunshine the baby brought and the shadows it left behind.

Shoes are not a new institution, for way back in Genesis 14:23 we find that Abraham spoke of the laces of the shoes worn by the king of Sodom. Throughout the Scripture—from Genesis clear through to Ephesians—they are used as types and pictures of truths that are precious to our heart.

There are shoes with spikes which are used on the field of games. There are delicate, dainty shoes of silver and of gold decorated with jewels which are worn in palaces of kings. There are rough, heavy shoes built for mountain climbing. There are heavy, leaded shoes which the diver wears in descending to the depths of the sea. Special, lightweight shoes are made for the runner in the race. Some shoes are fur-lined for the journeys into the far north. Other shoes are made of open-work materials for the extremely hot weather. There are shapely, well-fitted shoes for the businessman, and gaudy, fancy shoes for the giddy girl. I have seen wooden shoes which are worn in Holland. There are also gum shoes which are worn by the fishermen.

Let us now consider some of the lessons which are taught us by a study of these interesting articles of wear. How strange it was that Joshua and all the great and wise men of Israel should be so badly fooled by a pair of shoes! In Joshua 9:5 and 13 we read that the Gibeonites came before the generals of the army of Israel wearing old worn-out shoes with which to deceive Joshua. They pretended that the shoes had been worn out by the long journey which they had made. How could their shoes wear out when they had asses on which to ride? How could they wear out a pair of shoes on one journey anyway? How could these shoes fool a people who are experts in the shoe business? These old shoes were the downfall of the people of Israel and for many years brought about a terrible drought in the land because of the wicked heart of King Saul.

In the beautiful book of Ruth where we read the love story of Ruth and Boaz, a shoe played a prominent part in this romance. The relative who should have taken Ruth for his bride was unwilling to do so. We read the story in Ruth, chapter 4, verses 6 to 8. The unwilling kinsman removed the shoe from his foot and gave it to the judge. This was a public denunciation of his kinsman rights and his public refusal to accept Ruth as the sweetheart of his life. Boaz was glad enough to get the shoe, for with the shoe he got the lovely girl as well. Ruth became his bride and the grandmother of King David and one of the ancestors, from the human standpoint, of Jesus. I hope that Boaz put that shoe in a glass case and preserved it for his posterity.

Shoes should not be worn in the presence of God. Moses was told to remove his shoes when in the presence of the Lord at the burning bush (Exod. 3:5). Joshua was required to remove his shoes when in the presence of the Man with the drawn sword (Josh. 5:15). Isaiah was required to remove his shoes as well, at the command of God (Isa. 20:2).

Our Lord knows how to preserve shoes. For in Deuteronomy

29:5 we learn that the Lord preserved the shoes of Israel for forty years while they traveled through the desert. What a miracle this was! Dry, hot sand is always injurious to leather. The oil is taken out of the skins by the heat. The grinding of the particles of sand destroys the texture. The long tramping would injure both the stitches and the substance of the material. The preserving of these shoes is a wonderful proof of the miracle-working power of God.

Some strange shoes are mentioned in Deuteronomy 33:25, "Thy shoes shall be iron and brass." These would not be soft but they would be safe. They would not insure comfort but they would endure hardness. The fact that God gave them would indicate that He knew how rough the road would be. Iron is for durability and brass is for beauty. Although the way would be long and the road would be rough and the obstacles would be great, God promised His people that He would fit their feet for the journey.

Sometimes the Lord smoothes the roads, levels the hills, removes the rough places and leaves our feet shod with soft sandals. Other times He leaves the road as it is, not changing it a bit, but He equips His pilgrim with feet and with shoes that can safely and securely travel the roughest ways. Either method is quite all right. Both cases glorify His name and bless the weary wanderer on the way Home.

Our Lord describes beautiful feet if they have the proper shoes. In Song of Solomon 7:1 we read, "How beautiful are thy feet with shoes."

No one seems to be proud of the feet. Advertisements describe beautiful eyes and attractive teeth, but whoever read of beautiful feet. Our Lord has provided for beautiful feet by saying, "Your feet shod with the preparation of the gospel of peace" (Eph. 6:15). Of these He writes in Romans 10:15, "How beautiful are the feet of them that preach the gospel of peace."

Would you think that a pair of shoes would be worth more than a man? We read in Amos 2:6, "They sold the righteous for silver, and the poor for a pair of shoes." Human life is not very valuable when the grace of God is excluded from the heart. The beautiful traits of character, which we love to see in men, come from the heart of God and are imparted by the Holy Spirit.

Let us trust ourselves, our souls and our sins to Christ Jesus the Lord, that He may fit our feet for the path of life.

The Dandelion is Unusual

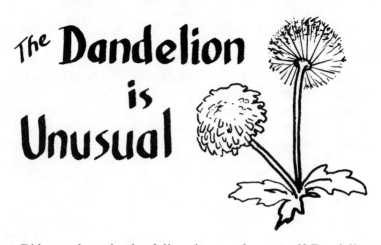

Did you plant the dandelions in your front yard? Dandelions are no respecters of persons. They adorn the yards of the rich and show their yellow glory around the hovels of the poor. They delight to grow in the cemetery or in the garden of the prince. They flourish in the woods where no one can observe them, or they show their smiling faces right near your front steps though they certainly will be dug up at the first opportunity.

How persistent they are! How quickly they develop! They are up in the morning before you are. They blossom and go to seed and seed your neighbor's lawn while you are trying to make up your mind whether to dig them out yourself or hire someone else to do it. They are the first to bloom in the Spring, and the last to be discouraged in the Fall.

Let us consider the message which the dandelion gives to us. We, too, should be out early with the seed of the Word of God and continue until the shadows fall, scattering the message.

If the grass in your front yard is two inches high, the dandelion will grow three inches. If you should neglect to cut the lawn and the grass grows five inches long, the dandelion will grow six inches high and smile in the sun. If you should be on a vacation and the grass should grow ten inches long, then that persistent, "not-to-be-whipped" dandelion will grow eleven inches tall and stick up its nose at the passing throng. It simply will not be downed. It rises above "its circumstances." It will not be outdone by its neighbors. It has an ambition to get somewhere and it gets.

One dandelion plant may multiply itself by several hundreds. Quite a few blooms will appear from the one plant and on each bloom there will be many seeds. Each seed is equipped with a sail to carry it on the wind. The Lord knew that no one would plant dandelions and that men would despise them, so He gave them the means of quickly recovering from the devastating knife of man by causing them to multiply quickly and profusely. The seeds ripen very quickly and a puff of wind blows them over the entire neighborhood.

So the Lord would have us to be fruit-bearing children of His. It is those who "turn many to righteousness," who shall shine as the stars forever and ever. The Father is glorified if ye bear MUCH fruit.

The dandelion is not easily discouraged. It does not wilt with sorrow because it has to bloom behind the barn. It does not hide its face with shame because it cannot be on the front lawn of the courthouse. It does the bidding of its Maker happily and beautifully, whether it is in an obscure place or in a very prominent garden.

Our Lord would have us to serve just as well among the poor or among the rich; we should serve as gladly and as efficiently with the few as before the many. We should not care at all for those who observe us but only for the pleasure of Him who sent us.

Just as the dandelion knows no season, so the servant of God should be "in season, out of season." When the world thinks that the Gospel is out of season, the Christian must know that it is in season. When the world thinks the Scriptures are out of place, the believer must know that the Word of God is always in place. There is no time that is out of season for the precious Word of the living God.

The diligence of the dandelion should be a challenge to our hearts. It is often growing and doing the will of its Maker while God's children are growing and living in disobedience. The dandelion is busy producing the flower for beauty and the seed for service, while some of God's saints are busy cultivating ugly habits and destroying the seed that others have sown. The dandelion does what its Master equipped it to do, while sometimes the Christian is busy doing the things he should not do.

Dandelions always tell the same golden story. Whoever heard of a blue dandelion? They bring that golden yellow up out of a black soil. They smile at you in the cold, gray morning and bid you a golden greeting at night, when you come home weary with the work of the day.

How like this we should be! Why should not the child of God show the golden glory of the Sun of Righteousness in his face constantly? We, too, should have a happy greeting for those whom we meet along life's road. They should see us and take courage. They should see our example of diligence and persistence and take new heart. Our presence and our actions should instill new hope in the hearts of those who observe us.

As the dandelion seeks out every nook and corner in which to grow and smile and prepare its seed, so should we constantly seek opportunities to bring the sunshine of God's love and the seed of His Word into every nook and corner in the community where we live.

What a fertile spot every place presents! Sometimes we sow the seed in the jail and sometimes in the orphan's home. It may be in the home of a neighbor where we shall show the flowers and fruits of God's grace, or it may be in the office and the shop. Everywhere the soil is ready, waiting for the seed. We are to be sowing early and late, permitting the Holy Spirit to blow our message into every heart where He would have it go.

The beautiful golden yellow of the dandelion comes from the dark, damp soil. How can black dirt produce a beautiful blossom? Ah, that is one of God's mysteries. Only God can do it. Only God would do it. It is a miracle which we often see in nature and also in society. Out of the dark ground comes the white hyacinth, the yellow rose, the blue cornflower, the purple violet, the tinted lily, and the golden dandelion.

Out of the foul and the filth of sin, God has brought many a man and many a woman who adorn His doctrines and who exemplify the glories of His great grace. Men who were a curse in the home have been changed into a benediction. Men whose mouths were foul and filthy with liquor, tobacco, and oaths have been made into vessels of glory whose mouths were filled with His praises. Men who were a curse to society have been transformed into the greatest of blessings. Yes, our God can bring beautiful things out of horrible things, if only we will trust our souls and our lives to Him.

Dandelions care for neither the smiles nor the frowns of men. Their business is to bloom and they do it. Their work is to seed the soil and they accomplish it remarkably well. Their business is to work early and late, and they never take a vacation.

The Lord help us to be like the dandelion.

Opals and Butterflies

The remarkable transformations that take place in nature are worthy of our careful attention and serious consideration. We shall be impressed with the fact as we consider some of these, that there is a personal, living God who alone can produce such miracles.

In the animal kingdom, in the vegetable kingdom, and in the mineral kingdom, we shall find strange things taking place which we cannot explain but must believe without understanding them. Some mysteries cannot be solved. Most of nature's mysteries remain mysteries. We see the results, we enjoy the facts, but we cannot fathom the why-for nor the where-for.

The **caterpillar** (an upholstered worm) slowly crawls along with its fourteen or more legs. It is covered with hair that is yellow or white or brown. It eats green things with its tiny mouth and has no interest in beautiful flowers, nor the sweet nectar that lies within the heart of those blooms. It makes no effort to fly but is content with crawling. It makes no show of gaudy colors but is content to be plain.

As winter draws nigh this peculiar little thing begins to weave a coffin around itself, beginning at the rear end and weaving forward. Finally it encloses itself completely in a casket that is waterproof, sunproof and unsinkable. Through the terrible cold of the winter it remains enclosed in its little house.

When the springtime comes with its warm sunshine, in some peculiar, mysterious way which I have not been able to understand, a ragged hole appears in one end of this casket and soon there emerges, not the worm that entered with its yellow hair and its many feet, but a beautiful butterfly with wonderful brilliant color, six legs, and a long peculiar tongue with which it may draw up the nectar of the flowers. Only God could bring about such a great change.

How does the butterfly get out? Does anyone know? What became of all those other legs and where did the hair go, for the butterfly has tiny scales, one million to the square inch?

The God who can accomplish this wonderful miracle can transform your life and make it wonderful if you will let Him have it.

Opals are dug from the deep recesses of the earth. We are told that God takes a handful of sand and buries it deep in the ground where the terrific heat from beneath and the tremendous weight from above will transform it into the beautiful stone we admire so much and which we call the opal. Tradition has it that the opal in some way affects the fortunes of life. This, of course, has no foundation or fact, for God rules the destinies of men and an opal can only enhance the beauty of its owner. The opal really has no color of its own, but has the unusual ability to radiate the various colors from the sunbeams causing it to flash like fire.

Only God can make an opal and only God can make you reflect the beauties and the glories of Christ Jesus the Lord.

The sapphire is a beautiful stone and is the birthstone for September. This beautiful gem seems to be a product of clay. The living God, who made the clay originally, may have taken a handful, deposited it deep in the bowels of the earth where it would be subject to intense heat and a great pressure, so that when men by laborious digging should find it, it would have been transformed into a beautiful gem fit for the crown of a king.

There are many colors in sapphire stones. Some are a beautiful "corn-flower" blue and are unusually valuable. Others are yellow and are known as golden sapphires. Violet sapphires have been found and others with a bright orange color. This is a very expensive sort and most of them come from Ceylon across the sea.

Only God can make a sapphire, and only God can transform the common sinner who is like the common clay into an uncommon Christian, prepared for the Palace of Glory. Let Christ have you and He will transform you too.

The diamond is the most fascinating stone of all. How strange it is that God should take black carbon, which is dark and dense, and by the transforming of lava heat and tremendous pressure, change that substance into the beautiful gem which adorns the bride's finger!

Most of the diamonds in the world have been found in South Africa, at Kimberly and at Diamantina and at Jagers Fontein and in other places. Geologists have found great deposits of lava in chimney-like formations which extend deep down in the earth where diamonds abound. All diamonds were one time lost. They have been found by searching men.

All sinners have been lost but some have been found by the seeking Saviour, have been rescued from the depths of darkness and despair, and have become the property of the King of kings.

Diamonds are always found "in the rough." They must be polished by the lapidary, and suitably set by a jeweler.

So our Lord takes the rough sinner and begins to polish him as a gem for His crown. Only He can do the polishing. Only He knows how much the stone can stand. Only He knows the best shape the stone should finally take. Only He knows the best setting, the best circumstances in which to place His gem.

The Lord will transform you, too, from carbon to diamond, from ugly black to beautiful, brilliant, striking colors, if only you will trust Him with your soul. Do it now.

The grub, which is a bug somewhat like the "Junebug" but smaller, crawls around in the mire and muck of a stagnant pond. Little does it care for the mud on the bottom of the swamp or the green scum on the top. Its joy and delights are in living there. It is unmindful of the glorious sunshine above, the singing birds round about, the beautiful flowers on the neighboring hills, the great trees around the bank.

One day a strange feeling possesses this queer little creature. It has an itching in its back and its whole body becomes restless with a strange desire to climb to the surface. It laboriously makes its way up the stalk of some reed or weed until near the surface. There it pauses for a while to rest. Suddenly by a peculiar motion of the body, the skin or the shell bursts open and there emerges a new and beautiful flying creature known as the dragonfly. How thin are its wings, like gauze! How beautiful are its colors, like the rainbow! How lightly it flies, like the sunbeam flickering here and there! It scorns the scum. It despises the darkened depths of the stagnant pond. It cares nothing for its former relatives, associates and friends who are still in the muck and the mud. It lives on a higher plane and enjoys the beauties of God's creations.

This is a beautiful picture of the great change brought about by the new birth of the soul. The wicked man lives in the mire of his sins and the filth of his passions until one day the Master Maker of men, Christ Jesus our Lord, finds him. The transformation is complete. Up he comes into the sunshine of God's love, to be graced with the gifts of Heaven. Oh, what a change!

Do let Him change you!

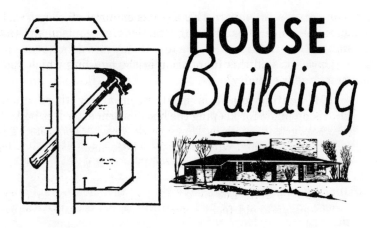

HOUSE Building

This peculiar question is asked by God in Isaiah 66:1, "Where is the house that ye build unto me?" The pride of the contractor is to build a house more beautiful, more strangely-constructed than others have built and in a situation that is unusually difficult.

Evidently our Lord expects each of us to build a house for Him in the place where we are and in the circumstances that surround us. Often the Christian is referred to as a builder, particularly in Paul's Epistles. Since the fact remains that each one is actually building something for eternity, it will be of interest and of profit if we shall consider some of the details of this work.

Jude uses the expression, "Building up yourselves on your most holy faith" (vs. 20). Let us proceed to do so. The first part of this building will be—

The foundation. No builder would proceed with the superstructure until he was assured that the foundation was sufficient and secured to a firm base.

The foundation in every man's life should be Jesus Christ, for we read in I Corinthians 3:11, "Other foundation can no man lay than that is laid, which is Jesus Christ." He is indeed the "Rock of Ages." Those who rest upon Him, put their trust in

Him, are saved and are safe. He has endured all the ages of the past and will still be a resting place for His people in all the ages to come.

Have you laid this foundation in the building which you are erecting for eternity?

The heating plant is most essential for there must be provision made for keeping the house warm after it is built. God wants warm Christians that are on fire for souls and whose hearts are warmed with His love. There should be no coldness in this building of ours. We should see to it that our hearts are always kept warm for Him. There should be a fervor in our love that can be felt. Let us guard against a cold heart in our devotions and cold feet in our service. Keep yourselves warm for God.

There must be a living room. The old-fashioned "sitting-room" with the open fireplace, the grandfather clock, the comfortable old rocking chairs and the dim light of the lamp invited many a visitor to a happy evening of sweet converse. It is in the living room that we entertain our friends and visitors. Hospitality is so valuable in God's sight that He speaks of some that were "given to hospitality" (Rom. 12:13). Paul urged the saints to use hospitality one to the other (I Pet. 4:9).

What lovely hours we have spent in the sitting room of a Christian friend talking together about the things of our Lord while sharing each other's burdens and joys! Be sure that you have a good large living room in your house, where you may entertain "angels unawares" and even some who are not so good as angels. Many a heart has been won by the sweet influences of the sitting room.

Upstairs there is a bedroom. We need rest. Everyone must rest. Nearly one-third of our whole time is spent in bed. Do you ever rest? The Lord Jesus said, "Come unto me, all ye that labour and are heavy laden, and I will give you rest" (Matt. 11:28).

Not only must we make provisions for resting our own weary hearts and burdened minds but we should provide resting places for others. The kind of a guest room you have reveals the kind of heart you have.

Do others come to you with their burdens? How sympathetic we should be. How willing we should be to bear the burdens of those who are carrying some heavy load. What an honor it is to lift the load from our brother's shoulder and let him rest a while! The busy servant of God needs to take time to rest apart from his labors. It was the Saviour who said, "Come ye yourselves apart into a desert place, and rest a while" (Mark 6:31). Have a good rest room in the mansion you are building for Him.

A bath is needed. We accumulate so much of soil and sin traveling through life that we must take time to slip away for cleansing. Sometimes things must be burned in the TRASH BURNER. Sometimes the bath will do it. Our house must be fully equipped with means for the removal of dust and dirt; of fault and failure; of sin and shame.

The blood of Christ and the Word of Christ are God's two remedies. Do you have them in the house that you are building?

A kitchen and a dining room are essential in this home of ours for we must feed on good food if we would be fat and flourishing for our Lord. Christ told Peter to "feed my sheep." He did not say "educate them," though education is valuable and profitable. Christian scholarship is to be commended and invited. It is not, however, vital and necessary.

Food is vital to the life. The Lord Jesus said, "He that eateth me, even he shall live by me" (John 6:57). The soul that is born of God must feed on bread from Heaven. Spiritual food out of the Word of God makes spiritual men more spiritual.

Are you feeding daily on the Bread of Life? Have you arranged for a dining room in your Spiritual Home?

A library must be provided. The Lord places no premium on ignorance. In this house which we build for His name we must provide for teaching and make room for learning. We are to grow in the knowledge of the Son of God. We are to study to show ourselves approved unto God. We are to learn the ways of the Lord, the Word of the Lord, the will of the Lord and the works of the Lord.

Knowledge is a fountain; knowledge gives strength; knowledge gives power. Intelligent Christians can do far more for God than ignorant ones. To know how to do God's work in God's way assures the blessing of God on the effort.

Let us study carefully the sixty-six books in God's library that we may be intelligent believers and educated servants of our Lord.

The music room will bring joy to the heart of God and man. Many Christians provide no music in a house which they are building for God. Singing is a sign of the Spirit-filled life. Singing is a proof of the presence of victory.

It was David's songs in the midst of his sorrows that drove away the shadows and made him more than a conqueror. It was when the singing began in the Temple that the glory of God filled the house. It was when the song of the Lord began in the forefront of the Army that God discomfited their enemies. Songs break down adamantine walls. Songs break stubborn hearts. Songs revive the drooping spirit.

Have you a music room in your house?

It Is Peculiar

The strange things in nature, which surround us daily and which we seldom notice, are of the greatest interest, and reveal the wonderful knowledge and wisdom of a personal God.

The mother opossum carries her babies on her back. There is very little hair on her body, and therefore the babies would have nothing to hold on to if they were on her back. God has made provision for this situation by teaching the mother to curl her long, stiff tail up over her back to her head. The babies jump up on each side of her back and curl their tails around her tail. In this way there will be four or five of the babies hanging securely on each side of the mother's body. Those on one side counterbalance the weight of those on the other side.

Who taught the opossum this trick? Is there a school in which opossoms are trained? Did some great atheist or infidel suggest this method of transportation to the opossum family and teach them to do it?

The lark is perhaps the most beautiful of all singing birds. The bird itself is not so attractive but its song baffles description. Many poems have been composed about the entrancing strains that emanate from this little throat. Many stories have been told of its wonderful song. In all of these poetic efforts, however, nothing is said about the feet of the lark. No one would ever sing about the lark's feet. They are ugly and quite out of proportion in size. The toes are unusually long and are covered with rough, unsightly growths.

Did God make a mistake when He gave the lark her beautiful voice, so exquisitely rich, yet gave her such unsightly feet? No, God always doeth all things well. The lark does not build a nest but lays her two eggs on the ground in some small depression, perhaps at the edge of the field or of a pasture. If any danger should arise whereby her eggs might be destroyed, she picks up those two eggs in her two feet and flies away with them, to deposit them in a place that would be more safe from intruders. Her toes are extra long so they can enclose the egg without crushing it, and are made horny and rough so the egg will not slip out and fall.

The God who thus cares for the little lark cares more deeply for you. Why not trust Him with your problems?

The peculiar gait of the elephant has no doubt attracted your attention as it swung along the street in the circus parade. It seemed so cumbersome and awkward in its movements, yet it may be that you did not discover the reason.

The elephant, as you know, has the largest and the heaviest body of any living animal. Other animals are able to rise from the ground on two legs. The cow, whose hind legs bend backward, lifts its body first on its hind legs, then completes its rising motion by the front legs. The horse, whose hind legs also bend backward, reverses the operation. It rises first on its front legs, then completes the job by lifting the remainder of its body with the hind legs. Why do these two animals not rise from the ground in the same way? What light does the hypothesis of Darwinian evolution shed on this peculiar characteristic?

The hind legs of the elephant are quite unlike the hind legs of other quadrupeds in that they bend forward just like the front legs. The wise provision of God was rendered necessary because of the great weight of the body. The elephant could not lift the tremendous weight on two legs alone. It must use all four of its legs to lift so many pounds to an upright position.

The God who fitted the elephant to carry its burden is able to fit you to carry yours. Will you let Him?

Migratory birds change their habitat with the seasons. In the

97

Autumn the birds from the North fly to the warm sunny South. In the Spring these same birds return to their northern feeding grounds to remain for the Summer season. It must be noted with much interest that myriads of fish in the northern waters of the ocean swim to the southern seas and the warmer habitat at the very same time that the birds begin to fly to the southern clime.

How can the birds and the fish prognosticate? How do they know what is coming in the next few weeks? To what schoolroom did they go in order to learn geography? They have no navigation instruments either for air or for water, yet they will return to the very location from which they left. The God who made them, the Lord who endowed them with instinct, a living personal God who is wonderfully working, He only can perform such a miracle. Let Him give you His new nature through saving faith in Jesus Christ His Son.

The seawater is filled with salt. Many of the fish which we eat are taken from this salt water. Have you ever noticed that none of these fish are salty? All fish taken from the ocean must be salted at the table, or at the cannery, before the meat is tasty and fit to eat. Why is it that a fish can live all its life in salt water, yet none of the salt gets into it? That is just another touch of God's handiwork.

The Christian is reminded by this incident that though we live in the world, we are not of the world, and the world should not be in us. We may live many years in the very midst of the world with its pleasures, its attractions, its allurements, yet be wholly separated unto God.

Do you know who teaches the bird to build a nest? The baby birds were not around when Mother built the nest in which they were hatched. I have never seen baby birds receiving instructions on nest-building. I do not know of any college professor who specializes in teaching birds to build nests. I did observe one day a sparrow trying to begin the construction of a nest under the eaves of the house near my window. The wind was blowing that day in fitful gusts. As fast as she would bring a bit of yarn, or a piece of grass up to the beam, the wind would blow it away.

The little bird was not to be whipped in this manner, and I saw her do an unusual thing. She brought a bit of grass up to its place and stood on it as the gust of wind blew. Then she quickly darted down for another piece and thus she performed between the gusts of wind, until the nest was formed and anchored. She learned this trick from the God who doeth all things well.

A bird which has been hatched in an incubator and which has never seen a nest nor another bird will build a perfectly good nest of the sort which is built by its kind, and will lay her unfertile eggs in that nest. No wonder Job's pride was humbled when God said to him, "Doth the hawk fly by thy wisdom?" (Job 39:26), and, "Doth the eagle mount up at thy command, and make her nest on high?" (Job 39:27).

God performs an engineering feat which man would like very much indeed to understand. A limb nine inches in diameter will grow straight out from a tree thirty-two inches in diameter, projecting fifty feet, and weighing a thousand pounds. Several men could sit on this limb adding another thousand pounds of weight. The fibres of this limb do not penetrate the tree more than half its diameter, which would be sixteen inches.

Do you know of any engineer who could devise, or any material which could stand the strain if man should seek to duplicate this? If this secret could be discovered a bridge could be thrown across the Hudson River by anchoring only to one side.

"How marvelous are thy works, O God!"

The Best Robe

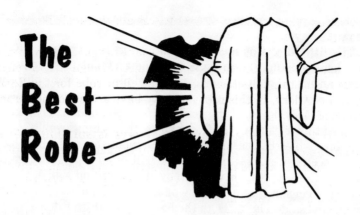

"Bring forth the best robe, and put it on him. . . ."—Luke 15:22.

Since our Lord called this the best robe, it must be in contrast with other robes which are not so good. We will therefore consider other robes in their relationship to this robe and see what our Lord may have meant by this peculiar and interesting statement.

This robe is the best robe **because it is free.** All other garments must be purchased. Some robes are quite inexpensive, while those which are worn by the king and queen at their coronation are lavishly expensive.

The robe of righteousness which the father gave to his prodigal son was a gift to his boy. No one can purchase this robe. It is the free gift of God. It is this robe referred to in Isaiah 61:10. It was made in Heaven and is the gift of Heaven's King, as were the wedding robes described in Matthew 22:10 and 11. No religion on earth can make such a robe. No man on earth has the right or the power to sell this robe.

It is the best robe **because it may be worn beyond the grave.** All other robes must be left behind. How often the widow is called upon to dispose of the garments left by her companion at his death. One robe accompanies him to the grave. All the others must be disposed of to relatives and friends who remain behind.

This BEST ROBE is received by the believer when he trusts his soul to Jesus Christ and he wears it through life, through death, and through eternity. It is the right robe for the Royal Court of Glory. In this robe one may have access to the throne room of God.

It is the best robe **because it always is suitable for the occasion**. A bathing suit would be out of place in the pulpit. A wedding dress would hardly be the style for a funeral. A diver's suit would not be suitable for the race track. A tuxedo would hardly be serviceable in a coal mine.

This robe of righteousness, however, which is called the best robe, is in style everywhere. It may be worn on the beach, or in the court of law. It is appropriate in school and in the store. It is quite "in place" at a wedding or at a funeral. It should be worn always at every place, on every occasion.

It is the best robe **because it always fits.** Other robes need to be changed with the changing years. Baby dresses give way to those of more mature sort. Knee breeches give way to long pants. Those who are slender may become portly and need a change both of style and dimensions in their garments. Those who are short may grow taller and the robe must be lengthened. This lovely robe of righteousness, the gift of God, needs no alterations. It may be received in youth and worn till the gray hairs appear. It always fits, no matter what other changes take place.

It is the best robe **because it is always in style**. There was a day when hoop-skirts were worn by society matrons. Who wants a hoop-skirt now? Balloon sleeves were once the height of fashion but no one would wear them now. Cotton clothes were once the style, but now they can hardly be found in the stores.

Styles change with the generations but the style of this best robe never alters. It is the same now as when it was first given by Christ. It was worn in Paul's day, in the days of the Wesleys; it was worn by John Knox and by Spurgeon. Through the centuries this robe of righteousness has remained unchanged.

It is the best robe **because it never needs repairs.** Most garments show the wear and tear of daily use. The sleeves become frayed, the buttonholes become raveled. The collar becomes soiled and worn. Many washings fade the colors. The garment wears through at the places where it is most rubbed. The cloth becomes tender with age and hard service.

It is not so with the best robe. It comes from Heaven and is maintained by Heaven. Those wear it best who love it most. Prayer, Bible reading and Christian fellowship keep it bright, neat and fresh.

It is the best robe **because of its great cost.** All robes of human manufacturers are produced at a price, but this robe of righteousness, this Best Robe, is priceless. Most other robes are obtained with no suffering. The sheep is sheared. The cotton is picked. The silk is gathered. This Best Robe has come from the terrible suffering of Christ Jesus our Lord.

Its warp and its woof are from Calvary. It is dyed with the precious blood of Christ. It is a product of His death on the cross. It cost Him His throne in Glory, the song of the angels, the adoration of the heavenly hosts. He willingly left it all to be an outcast. Through His sacrifice we receive this wonderful coat, this Best Robe.

It is the best robe **because no one can take it from you.** Sisters borrow each other's dresses. Brothers borrow each other's coats. Sons borrow the garments of their father. Just when you want your best garment for the party, some member of the family has taken it and left for some other function.

No one can take this robe from you. You wear it day and night. You wear it at work and at play. You wear it Sundays and holidays as well as every other day in the week. It is your own to have and to hold forever. It is your private property. It is your sacred treasure. Satan himself cannot take it from you.

It is the best robe **because it is always becoming.** Some folks cannot wear blue. Others look terrible in red. Some prefer green.

Whoever you are, whatever color your hair may be, or your eyes, this robe will beautify you. Your body may not be attractive. Your nose may be too large or your chin may recede too much or you may have a double chin. It matters not what your physical appearance may be. This robe of Heaven, this Best Robe, will be exactly the right robe for you. If you will accept Jesus Christ by faith just now, He will clothe you with it and you will be fitted for His presence.

We Should Be Thankful...

. . . Because we do not have universal joints at our elbows. How would Mother lift the skillet from the stove if the elbow joint did not have a "stopper" on the back side to keep the arm from going all the way back? Have you been thankful that your knee is not a universal joint? How would you ever stand upright or walk if there was not a "stopper" to keep the knee from bending all the way?

How thankful we should be because our teeth are made to match. You had nothing to do with it—neither did your good mother. The President never planned it in any of his progressive programs. It just happened that way because a loving, personal God, a thinking God, a God who knew how, has ordained that people should be born that way.

The teeth are arranged in exactly the right way. You could hardly chew corn from a cob with molar teeth. You certainly could not bite through some of the steaks being offered us today with wisdom teeth. Wisdom would tell you not to try it!

Do you not think that God was very kind when He placed your nose on your face up-side down? If your nose were turned right-side up, then every time it rained you would drown, and every time you should sneeze, it would blow your hat off! God never intended the nose to be a dust-catcher, so He placed it in the right position.

Only God could make an organ of taste. By the tongue, you can tell whether the substance you place in the mouth is

104

strawberry or pumpkin pie—whether it is potatoes or plums. The taste remains the same all through life, and in every part of the world. Strawberries and watermelons never taste like apples.

What a mess we would be in if vegetables, fruits, grains and meats should change their taste every year, or should taste differently in different parts of the world. Only God can preserve this condition, and only a living, personal God who loves us could or would have given us an organ of taste which could differentiate the different kinds of food.

The farmer should bow his head in thanksgiving because he does not need to plant all of his seeds right-side up. What a job he would have placing each grain in the ground in the proper position. He never would get the job done, nor could he hire enough people to do it in a satisfactory manner.

The living Lord has placed in each seed that peculiar thing which we call "instinct," so that the seed never gets confused about directions, but always "comes up." Whoever heard of a seed growing in the wrong direction? All seeds of every kind may be placed in the ground in any position; and they will certainly find their way up to the light. If God should fail to do this just once, in any one season, what a catastrophe it would be for the world!

The kindness of our wonderful Lord is revealed in the fact that He has made our bodies with a "one shot system." You put the food in your mouth, and get lubricating fluid in all the joints of the body. How would you like to rise each morning and grease all your joints? You never would get to work on time, and Mother never would have breakfast ready. You would squeak at every move because you would certainly forget some of the joints. What a bedlam we would have in the schoolroom because many of the lazy children would never take care of their joints. God has taken care of this need by letting us put all the necessary ingredients in one place—the mouth. He has arranged the body to take care of all the joints, the nerves, and every other part.

We are a thankless lot. We grasp after and grab every good

thing that God has to offer and usually we take it for granted; and forget.

The important blood vessels of the body and the principal nerve trunks are placed safely on the flexor, or inside places of the arms and legs, as well as in deep-seated places in the rest of the body. A wise and understanding God knew the hazards on the road of life and arranged special protection for these parts which are so essential for life.

Do you know why or how or when the human heart gives its first beat? There is a time in the life of the unborn child when there is no heartbeat whatever. The heart is just being formed. The parts are not complete. Then, one day, that heart, tiny as it is, gives its first beat. Why does it do it? What makes it do it? The mother had nothing to do with it, nor the father. Certainly the child does not bring it about by any will power of his own. The great men of earth do not cause it to happen—no laws have been passed in any country to govern it.

God starts it. Only God will stop it. The God who made it—the God who starts it beating, and the God who will stop its beating wants you to let Him have that heart of yours.

We should be thankful for the goodness of God in providing so richly for both the body and the soul. He has given us wool, cotton, linen, silk, and leather whereby the body may be clothed, preserved from heat and cold, and equipped for the conditions of life. He has given us grains, vegetables, fruits, meats, and liquids for the sustenance of the body that we may be well, strong, and healthy. He has given us educational facilities, arithmetic and all other mathematics, all forms of languages, music, physical training, sciences and arts, that we may live intelligently, act efficiently, and serve successfully.

All of these should lead us to want from His gracious and loving hand the provision He has made for our souls. The Word of the Lord is to teach us His will. The work of the Lord is to reveal His mind. His Son is to cleanse us from our sins. Trust Him.

The
BIGGEST
HANGING
of all

The story of any hanging usually gets a place on the front page of the paper. Man has been hanging his fellow man for centuries. It has been a common mode of execution and punishment. Kings have hanged other kings. Rulers have hanged traitors. Men have committed suicide by hanging. All of these instances are found recorded in the Bible, but none of these is "The Biggest Hanging."

It is recorded in Genesis 40:22 that Pharaoh hanged his chief baker because he found him guilty of a conspiracy against the throne. Men punish evildoers and perhaps the most serious of all crimes is that of being a traitor to the ruler of the country. Those who are traitors to God and enemies of Jesus Christ will receive a worse punishment than ordinary sinners. But this was not "The Biggest Hanging."

We find that Joshua, the great general of the armies of Israel, executed his enemies by hanging. In Joshua 8:29 he hanged the King of Ai on a tree, and in chapter 10 at verse 26 he hanged five great kings on trees, after he had whipped their armies and conquered their kingdoms. Even this was not "The Biggest Hanging."

An accidental hanging is recorded in II Samuel 18:10. A certain soldier came to Joab, David's commander-in-chief, and said, "Behold, I saw Absalom hanged in an oak." Absalom was the son of King David, engaged in a war of rebellion against his

107

father. He and the unfaithful army of David were engaged in battle with his father David and the faithful soldiers who remained true to David. Absalom was leading his troops and was riding upon a mule. As he was charging through the thick woods his mule went under the boughs of a great oak, and his head was caught in the oak in some manner. Whether his neck was fastened in a crotch of the branches, or whether his long heavy hair became entangled in the limbs, we do not know. It is clear that the mule kept on going, leaving Absalom hanging in the air by his head. Probably Absalom's hair, which was the source of his pride, was the cause of his defeat. Joab and his men found Absalom hanging there, and soon killed him with their darts. "Pride goeth before a fall." That wherein he gloried was the means of his destruction. Neither would we call this "The Biggest Hanging."

The great Ahithophel, a wonderful counselor and a man of unusual wisdom, ended his life by committing suicide through hanging himself. The story of this tragedy is recorded in II Samuel 17:23 and reads, "And when Ahithophel saw that his counsel was not followed, he saddled his ass, and arose, and gat him home to his house, to his city, and put his household in order, and hanged himself, and died."

He was careful to fix up his home, but was careless about fixing up his heart. He arranged his affairs in this life, but neglected the affairs of the next life. How sad it is that a man so great should have such a shameful death. Not all, who start well, end well. Neither was this "The Greatest Hanging."

A woman was the cause of the hanging of eleven men. She was a beautiful girl named Esther. Haman and his ten sons had conspired to bring about the death of the queen and all the queen's people, the Jews. The plot was discovered and made known to the king. Haman had built a gallows, seventy-five feet high, on which to hang Mordecai, who was the uncle of Queen Esther. When the king discovered Haman's wickedness, and his evil intentions against the queen, the decree went forth from the king's lips that Haman should be hanged on his own gallows.

The decree was executed and is recorded in Esther 7:10. It is quite evident that Haman's sons agreed with their father and so these ten young men were hanged also. And this is described in Esther 9:14. This was a great hanging and quite unusual because a father and his ten sons were hanged for one offense. This, however, was not "The Biggest Hanging."

Judas the traitor hanged himself after he betrayed Jesus. The sad end of this "man of opportunity" is told in Matthew 27:5. Judas had been close to Christ but never loved Him. Judas had served Christ but never accepted Him. Judas had been in Christ's company but never let Christ into his heart. Judas was called a disciple, but he followed the money instead of The Man. Judas' hanging was not "The Biggest Hanging."

On Calvary two thieves were hanged, but these were really nailed to the cross. We would hardly call this a hanging in the strict sense of the word. They were hanging there by the nails and suffered for their sins, as everyone must do.

The Biggest Hanging of all hangings is the first hanging recorded in the Bible. Job, who lived in Abraham's day, wrote, "He stretcheth out the north over the empty place, and hangeth the earth upon nothing" (Job 26:7). Did you notice what He hung it on? He made the earth out of nothing and then God hung it upon nothing. Did you notice carefully those words? Only a real, personal, individual, living, intelligent God could make the myriads of things on earth out of nothing, and then hang them over an empty space upon nothing.

Do you really believe that He did it? Perhaps you folk who say there is no personal God, or no individual God, would like to explain how an "idea" or "mind" or "truth" or "love" or "infinite" or any other abstract nonentity could make the earth out of nothing and then hang it upon nothing.

There are ninety-two basic chemical elements which, in their various forms and combinations, form this earth. God has made gold for beauty, and aluminum for lightness, and iron for strength. God has combined these elements with other elements to give us grains, vegetables, fruits, flowers and a myriad of other products. God took nothing and made something. Then He took the something and hung it upon nothing. All of this is given to us to encourage our faith.

It is written in Romans 4:17, "God quickeneth the dead, and calleth those things which be not as though they were." It is also recorded in I Corinthians 1:28, "God hath chosen things which are not, to bring to nought things that are."

This is a wonderful message for the Christian heart. You do not need to have something with which God can begin to do something. You may have a very obscure life. You may have a very few gifts or talents. You may think you have no ability whatever. Just let the Holy Spirit have you in your weakness and with your emptiness and He will prove these passages to be true in your case.

If you are a lost sinner, wandering in the dark, with a heavy heart, you may come empty-handed and accept the Lord Jesus Christ to be the Lord of your life and the Saviour of your soul. You may come to Him with nothing. You will find in Him everything. Bring your problems to Him in your extremity. He can make something out of nothing.

The flag of the United States in a very peculiar way presents many interesting lessons which will be profitable for us to consider. We shall see that there are explanations which will be valuable to us in the construction of this lovely emblem of our country. Let us first consider them in their numerical order.

There is one flag, but it is composed of three colors, even as there is ONE GOD but THREE BLESSED PERSONS in that Godhead. These Three are separate from each other but are never separated from each other.

There are two parts to the flag—the field, where the stars appear, and the "fly" where the stripes appear. So there are two parts to our life—the Heaven of blue, where the righteous servants of God shall shine as the stars, and the scene on earth where stripes of sorrow and pain accompany every life.

There are three colors and these in union make our flag of liberty, but separated they tell a tragic story. There is the red of anarchy, there is the white of surrender, there is the blue of immobility. We do not want them separated, for together they represent justice and judgment, fellowship and friendship. It is so in the Godhead. God's justice and judgment are mingled with His mercy and grace. We do not want them separated.

There are four sides to this flag, even as we shall dwell in a city foursquare. To enter that city, we must be washed white in the red blood of the One who is now on His throne beyond the blue of the heavens.

Five points appear on each star. One of these points upward, two of them point outward and two point downward. We must be right with God before we can be right with our fellowmen and before our walk will be godly and good.

Five is the number of weakness in the Bible. Five fingers indicate that our hands are weak for many kinds of industry. Five toes remind us that our walk is not what we would like it to be. Five senses certainly indicate our need of more perception, more knowledge and better understanding. We shall never shine as stars with those perfect points unless we are made into God's stars by God's grace and through trusting the Lord Jesus Christ for salvation.

Six rows of stars and six white stripes bring to our attention the fact that man has been given sufficient provision both for his body and his soul. Six in the Bible is the number of man's consummation. Six days were given to Israel in which to finish their work. There were six steps to Solomon's throne for he had sufficient judgment ability to handle every case. The six white stripes are divided into three short and three long. White in the Bible is sometimes used to indicate the presence of leprosy; the short stripes indicate that some are little sinners while the long ones represent old sinners.

The seven red stripes beautifully indicate to us that there is enough power in the blood for every kind of sinner. The red stripes are as long as the white stripes. The blood of Christ cleanses all the way from the cradle to the grave. Be sure that you are trusting in that precious blood of Christ. The flag is enclosed in red and we too must be wholly sheltered under the blood if we would be safe from coming wrath.

The eight rows of stars tell us that a new nation was formed and a new liberty offered to all those who come under the shadow and the shelter of this flag.

In the Bible the number eight has the significance of "A NEW

THING." David was the eighth son of Jesse and he began a new dynasty in Israel. Christ arose the eighth day and began a new church. The eighth note on the piano is the beginning of a new octave. The eighth day of the week is the first day of a new week.

The man who trusts Jesus Christ becomes a new man, sings a new song, has a new vision, is filled with new hope, rests upon a new foundation, finds new companionships, learns new truths from the Scriptures and is a new creature in Christ Jsus.

Under this flag, many divers kinds of people become amalgamated in the great melting pot of the United States and become brothers in citizenship with all racial and national barriers broken down. So it is in Christ. Those who come under the banner of His love lay aside their differences, racial, social, national and financial, and sit down together in sweet fellowship around the table of the Lord under His banner.

Those are protected, who belong to the commonwealth over which this flag flies as its national emblem. Our government will preserve both the property and the persons of those who belong to our country. Those who belong to the living God, who are saved by grace, are kept by the power of God and preserved by the love of God and are surrounded by the mercy of God wherever they may be in the whole world.

This flag should be displayed by those who own it, and confess their citizenship under it; even so the Christian is called upon to confess Christ before men, own that God is his Father, Christ is his Saviour, the Spirit is his Guide, the Bible is his authority. Let us openly and constantly confess that our citizenship in this world under the sovereignty of Satan has ceased and that now we are marching under the banner of the cross.

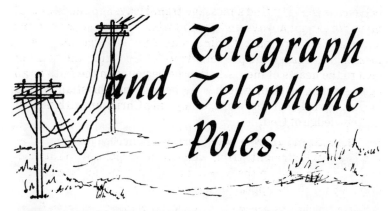

Telegraph and Telephone Poles

While riding across the country in Southern Kansas I was impressed with the peculiar appearance of the telephone poles along each side of the road. Some were long, others were short; some were crooked while others were straight. Some were quite large, others were saplings. Some seemed to have been manufactured by man, others were the natural growth out of the woods.

I asked myself, "What lessons may be learned from these strange poles which are in the service of my fellowmen?" The following thoughts presented themselves to me.

The telephone pole is dead. While it was a living tree in the forest it was not in the service of man. It must die if he could use it where he wanted and as he wanted.

The sinner living his own natural life in the world is not much of a servant for God. He is planning his own life; he is arranging his own affairs; he is living for himself. If kneeling at Calvary he will die with Christ, then he will be a living servant of the living Lord and may then be fit to carry His messages.

The telephone pole carries a message. It does not understand the message, it is not interested in the message; its purpose is to uphold that line through which the message is being taken to its destination. Any kind of a pole can do this. The message is not dependent upon the character of the pole but only upon the service which it renders. So the business of the

114

believer is to carry God's message from Heaven to the hearts of men. We cannot always understand what our Lord has said; the ways of God are past finding out. Any believer may be a messenger to carry the precious Word of God from the heart of God to the hearts of men, whether he be young in the faith or an aged servant of God, whether he be a great Christian with a large knowledge of the Word, or a young Christian with almost no knowledge of God.

"The natural growth pole" serves its purpose just as well as the beautiful, straight, trim, well-equipped pole. All that each one does is to hold up the wire, and the one does it as well as the other although the appearance is not so attractive.

Some Christians are well-trained, cultured, educated, refined. As they carry the message they may wear a full-dress suit; they may preach behind a solid mahogany pulpit; the floor of their platform may be carpeted with an imported rug; the members of their congregations may sit in cushioned pews. The message, however, which he may give will be only the message of the grace of God from the heart of God to those in his audience who hunger and thirst after righteousness.

Across the way there may be a smaller church where there are no carpets on the floor, and the grammar and rhetoric of the preacher would hardly get a passing mark in an examination. He may not know when to use "set" or "sit" nor when he should use "did" or "done." His congregation may be sitting upon improvised benches made of rough lumber. Coal-oil lamps may adorn the walls for lights, but his message may be the same precious words of life that are being given across the way in the palace of luxury.

Some of the poles were quite crooked while others were straight as a pencil. We find it so in Christian experience. Some whom our Lord raises up to carry His message have been reared in Christian surroundings where a holy atmosphere pervaded the home, godliness characterized the parents, and righteousness characterized the lives of the members of the family. His was not a wayward life. He never roamed the paths of sin. He was sheltered all his days by the shadow of the church. He carries a message from the Lord of Heaven and earth to the people of earth.

Another, however, may have been reared in surroundings of quite a different nature—the father a drunkard, the mother a brawling woman, and wicked influences may have surrounded him from the day of his birth. Ungodliness may have been the atmosphere of his home. Profanity, liquor, and lawbreaking may have characterized those with whom he associated.

Then one day the grace of God appeared, the light of the Gospel fell upon his heart, his soul was touched, his life was transformed by the sovereign grace of God. The precious blood washed him whiter than snow, and he became a bearer of the living message along the roadway of life.

Some of the poles I observed were quite short. Others were very long. At once I remembered some who had turned to the Lord in their youth and were given the privilege of bearing the message of grace only a few short years. Others saved in the early years of life were permitted to tell the story of redeeming love for many years. We never can tell how long we shall have the joy of testifying for our Lord. Our days may be shorter than we think. Their number may be less than we imagine. Let us carry the message well while we have the opportunity.

At the railroad track the poles were unusually long that the wires might not be damaged by the smoke and fire from the locomotive stack. God has always had some servants who were greater than others. They seem to reach up higher into the mysteries of Heaven than others; they are raised up for special purposes to reach a special kind of folk.

There must be some who can give the Gospel in the palaces of the kingdom, for all are not permitted to enter such places. Some must be raised up to tell of the Saviour's love to the princes of the business world and the kings of finance. God has them at His disposal. He plants them where He pleases. He lets them serve where they can bring Him the most glory.

These poles were separated to one service. They served

only one purpose, and they stuck to their job. Their work was to carry the wires through which the messages passed, and they were at the job day and night, never ceasing. They continued to serve winter and summer, in the storm and in the calm. Always they were in their positions holding up the living messages passing so swiftly through their hands.

We should be like that, never faltering, never failing, and always ready to be channels of blessing, upholding the Word of life. We should be in our places that others might get the message of blessing.

Some of these poles were injured by birds. Woodpeckers had eaten holes in their sides, the rain had entered, the rot had begun and the pole was weakened. To prevent this, the company in many instances had covered the poles with a preparation to keep out bugs and worms.

Should we not watch ourselves to see that the testimony is not weakened nor hampered nor hindered by the birds of sin? Pride, self-sufficiency, egotism, forgetfulness, laziness, personal ambition—these are the birds that would bore holes in our souls and make us poor vessels for the service of our King. We need to be preserved and protected from the decay and damage which this world attempts to inflict upon us.

These poles did not please themselves. A mastermind in the city assigned their location and determined the kind of poles to be used. Each pole lay dormant in the hands of its owner. The pole did not complain that it was out there alone at the roadside. It did not fuss because on each side of it there was a crooked pole and it seemed to be in bad company. It had only one job to perform and that was to stay where it was put and hold up the wires for its master.

Is it not the pleasure of our blessed Lord to plant His children where He wants them? Some would like a white-collar job, some would like special company, nicer, better, richer and finer than the ordinary run of life. If we would be like the telephone pole, however, we should be yielded to our Lord, quiet in our hearts, earnest in our efforts, ready and willing to carry the message even though it might be a lonesome place along the road of life.

The Story of the

POSTAGE STAMP

We may learn many interesting lessons from the postage stamp, particularly with regard to the Christian life, character and service. We shall consider each point with its relation to the daily life and see what profit we may gain from this meditation.

The stamp bears the imprint of the country in which it is of value and by which it was imprinted. The Christian life is not of any human origin but when truly presented by the godly man or woman it bears the print and the mark of Heaven.

The life of the Christian originated in the heart of God. The one who has been born again will be stamped by the Holy Spirit and with the life of Christ.

The stamp bears the mark of its value. Although the stamps may be the same size, they may be marked with a different price. The eight-cent stamp can do what the five-cent stamp cannot. The ten-cent stamp will carry a greater weight than the six-cent stamp.

All Christians do not have the same value to society and to the church. Some can usher at the door while others can hold a large audience spellbound for God. Some will scatter notices around the neighborhood inviting friends to the services while others will go to Africa to invite the natives to Christ.

Stamps are of various colors. Some stamps are red, some

are yellow, some are green, some are purple. Each color denotes either its value or its purpose. God has chosen five great colors for His children on earth—the yellow from the Orient, the brown from India, the black from Africa, the white from our own country, the red from the Indians in the desert. Each has his own peculiar characteristics. Each presents the Gospel in his own peculiar way. Each is of special use in his own particular sphere.

Some stamps have special purposes. The special delivery stamp is used for extra handling to expedite delivery. There is also "special handling"; this stamp is placed upon packages to insure rapid and special service at transfer points on the railroad. Revenue stamps are used for special tax purposes. "Postage Due" stamps are used to collect additional postage on a letter that is underpaid.

God has special Christians for special purposes. In I Corinthians, chapter 12, the Holy Spirit enumerates some of these gifts and in the history of the church we find them manifested. George Mueller had the gift of faith for the care and education of four thousand orphans. David Livingstone had the gift of faith for opening up Africa for the Gospel. John G. Paton had the gift of faith for entering the South Sea Islands among wild tribes of cannibals and leading them to the Saviour.

Have you asked what your special purpose in life is, and have you found it?

Stamps are made to use. The mucilage on the stamp is placed there to enable it to stick to its job until the end of the journey. The glue is the product of much labor and thought and is the result of much experimenting. It must not be poisonous for many stamps are moistened by the tongue. It must not get hard and dry, else it would not stick after lying around for some weeks.

The Lord expects His people to have this characteristic. Unstable folks are not much use to God. Stability, persistence, and dependability should characterize every Christian worker. If the Lord has placed in your hands some work for His glory, stay by it until it is done. Pursue it until it is finished. The Lord said about Reuben, "Unstable as water thou shalt not excel."

Some stamps are at a premium. Our government prints only a small issue sometimes. Because there are only a few, they are at once prized above the value which is printed upon them.

Often this is true of Christians. Because of their piety and their power they do more work and accomplish better results than many others. Some walk with God so closely that the few words they utter have unusual power and produce exceptional results. God does not make many Spurgeons nor many Moodys. These are men of exceptional value. God has chosen some women who have exceptional power in blessing others and remarkable ability in handling human problems.

Let our Lord make of you a special product designed for His glory and blessed in His service.

Stamps retain their value. It matters not when a stamp was printed. Its value remains unchanged so long as the government retains its power. When we purchase stamps we do not ask when they were printed. If we should find one among old papers in the desk we know it may be used, if it has never been cancelled. "Once a stamp, always a stamp" may be a good slogan.

It is so with the believer. Once he receives the imprint of Heaven, he remains the Lord's property and the Lord's servant ever after.

The stamp value is imputed. The paper on which the stamp is printed has almost no value whatever. A one-dollar stamp is printed on a bit of paper that would be worth less than one-tenth of one cent. The value does not lie in the article which is purchased at the post office window. We purchase an imputed value ordained by the government and placed on the stamp by their authority. The word of the government makes it worth one dollar, nothing else does.

It is the word of the living Lord that makes a common man a Christian. Christ pronounces the believing sinner a forgiven man. The Holy Spirit imprints upon the trusting soul the stamp of Heaven's life, and so righteousness is imputed and the man becomes a child of God.

Stamps are official in the country which issues them. Our stamps cannot be bought nor used in any other country. Those friends who would pass as citizens of Heaven must come out of Heaven's mint, must be born again, must be "official" in heavenly circles.

Do you bear the stamp of Heaven upon you?

The Silver Dollar

By means of the silver dollar, a contract may frequently be made with your banker. Let us notice the many lessons which may be learned from the inscriptions upon it.

On the obverse side there appears the head of the Goddess of Liberty, with the word "Liberty" appearing on the headband. Liberty comes only from Jesus Christ. He alone can break the chains that bind to sin and Satan. His truth alone can set us free from false doctrines and wicked teachings.

The date on the bottom is to ever remind us of the birth of Christ, for this silver dollar which bears the imprint of 1879 was made at the mint just that many years after the birth of Christ Jesus. The Lord will not let us forget that the Saviour came to save this banker.

A Latin inscription appears over the head of Liberty, "E Pluribus Unum." This is a foreign language and is indicative of the new language which is spoken by those who trust the Saviour and become newborn men in Christ. The thirteen letters in this inscription would bring before us that Christ and His twelve disciples began to give on earth this new message in a new tongue, which the world does not and cannot understand.

Thirteen stars appear also on this obverse side. The Lord would have us shine as stars forever and ever. He does not want us to waste our time, nor to misuse our talents. "Those who turn many to righteousness shall shine as the stars for ever and ever" (Dan. 12:3).

Seven stars are before the face of Liberty and six are behind her head. Natural talents are mingled with divinely-given virtues to enable us to become stars for His crown. The number six reminds us of the human talents received by birth and by education. The number seven tells us that our blessed Lord must make those gifts effective for Him or else we shall spend and be spent for our own selfish ends.

On the reverse side of this silver dollar, there appears an eagle with raised wings. The Scripture informs us, "Riches certainly make themselves wings; they fly away as an eagle toward heaven" (Prov. 23:5).

The talons of the eagle on the silver dollar are grasping both an olive branch and a group of arrows. Our Lord has arrows of vengeance for those who will not accept His olive branch of peace and mercy. He shows both to the world that we may accept of either one. His grace is free, but if it is rejected, then His judgment is compulsory.

The expression, "In God We Trust," appears over the head of the eagle. Eagles do trust in God, but all men do not. The God who made the eagle is the God to whom the eagle looks for her daily food and protection.

Our nation should trust in God. We will never be what we should be until our people and you in particular turn the heart to God in simple trust and in confident faith.

Near the bottom of the dollar is a tiny letter "S," or a letter "O," to indicate the mint which produced this coin. That soul which comes from God's mint should bear the impress of Heaven upon it. All should know who is our Maker and in what mold we have been patterned and formed.

At the bottom of this coin there are the words, "One Dollar." It advertises its value. People are entitled to know its value. This inscription prevents any misunderstanding. Every Christian has a value. Sometimes he values himself more highly than others esteem him to be worth. The value on this dollar was fixed by the government. We must take the standard which the government gives. Our own valuations have no place whatever in this matter. Let us ascertain what our value is

123

before God, then we may take that place before men.

Around the top of the dollar, these words appear, "United States of America." This is the testimony of the dollar as to its relationship. It constantly tells of its maker and original owner. It tells also where this dollar may be circulated and used. It is worth $1.00 in the United States of America and will pass for current money there.

We, too, must confess the One who has made us Christians and whose we are and whom we serve. Our ministry is in the kingdom of God and the church of His Son. Christians are at home in God's house and under His sovereignty.

An attractive wreath is gracefully curved about the eagle. This should be a call to our hearts to earn a diadem from our Lord. He has a crown to give and a wreath to bestow upon those who run the race well and who win the prize.

Soap is a product of Christianity. The heathen do not have soap. In some places a day's work may be obtained through the gift of a little soap. How would you like to live without soap? How difficult it would be to clean the body or to clean the dishes in the kitchen or to wash the clothing clean without this essential article of civilization! We forget to value it as we should because it is so common. In this short story we shall consider some interesting facts about it and learn some lessons from it.

Soap may be obtained in many forms. There are round cakes and oval cakes; there are long bars and short squares. It may be obtained in liquid form or in flakes. Sometimes it is furnished in powder and again like a jelly. It may be obtained in many colors: blue and green, white and yellow, red and brown.

Soap is often furnished, mingled with perfume to give it a beautiful scent. Some soap is made for hard water and some for soft water, but all of it is for cleansing purposes. Our Lord said in Jeremiah 2:22, "For though thou wash thee with nitre, and take thee much soap, yet thine iniquity is marked before me."

Soap has many uses. Surgical soap is found in the wash-up room of every hospital and is made with a germicide content for cleansing the hands before the operation. Other soap is of such a delicate nature that it is advertised for use on the tender skin of the baby. I have seen bars of soap made up with some kind of grit in its body for the removal of grease and very tenacious dirt, such as is found around machine shops. A special soap is made for killing body odors; sometimes the cure is worse than the disease. There is soap that dissolves very quickly and is used for dishwashing and for fine clothes. All of this soap, however, is just for cleansing purposes. Its presence affirms its need and announces the presence of dirt.

Just as it is necessary to use soap because we and our things become soiled, so it is necessary that the soul should be cleansed with some material which will effectively remove the stains that sin has made. The remedies that men manufacture for the removal of guilt and sin are likened to soap in Jeremiah 2:22. Soap will remove the dirt from the outside but cannot cleanse the inside. Soap is all right for what man can see but is of no value for what God can see. Soap will remove the dirt that men can reach but cannot cancel the guilt that only God can reach.

Our Lord is telling us in the above passage that after you have done all that you can with the best of human remedies and with an earnest intention, still the guilt remains and the stains are unremoved.

There are soaps on the market which are translucent; they are clear in their body and beautiful in appearance. Most soap is opaque. Some kinds of soap are made to float, while others sink to the bottom and are most difficult to find in the depths of the bath. Some soap is very expensive, while other varieties are exceedingly inexpensive.

Whether they be high-priced or cheap, none of them will avail to wash away the sins of the life and to cleanse the soul. "What can wash away my sin? Nothing but the blood of Jesus."

God has two remedies for the black marks of disobedience. The first is found in I John 1:7, "The blood of Jesus Christ his Son cleanseth us from all sin." The other is found in Psalm 119:9, "Wherewithal shall a young man cleanse his way? By taking heed thereto according to thy word." The blood of Christ cleanses the inward stains and the Word of Christ purifies the outward ways. These are God's cleansing agents.

Soap wears out with use and finally disappears in the water. Neither the precious blood nor the priceless Word have altered through the centuries. There is just as much value and efficacy now as there was in the beginning. The centuries have not altered nor weakened either one. There is still power in the blood, wonder-working power in the Word.

Children do not like soap. They must be begged and urged and compelled to wash with it. How often Mother has said, "Did you wash WITH SOAP?" Then while the reply was not confirmed by the appearance, Mother would smell the face to see.

As the child grows and perhaps a sweetheart comes into the life, soap becomes more necessary to the daily routine, and before the teenage has finished, the desire for cleanliness and the pride of appearance promote the use of soap rather freely.

It is so with God's remedies for sin—the blood and the Bible. As we become conscious of the stain upon the soul and of the spots which must appear to God as well as to men, we are constrained to appropriate God's blessed provision, the cleansing agents which He has provided.

Men have made their brands of soap famous by cleverly-worded sentences. "It floats" is known in every home in the land. "Keep that school-girl complexion" has made another soap famous far and wide. By repeating these statements over and over on billboards and magazines, in the daily press, over the air, the manufacturers have hoped, and successfully so, that their products would be accepted by all classes and nationalities.

Even so our Lord has made known far and wide by the printed page, by word of mouth, by the radio, on television, on advertising novelties, by pen and paint that "the blood of Jesus Christ his Son cleanseth from all sin." He, too, desires that every person in every class of every nation shall believe His advertising and shall accept this gracious means of cleansing.

All soap must be purchased. It does not grow on trees or bushes. It is not found in the sea nor in the soil. It must be produced by the skill and the art of men. This divine remedy for sin is not a natural product either. It came from the hands of God and is a product of Heaven. It is FREE. No one can buy it and no one can corner it. It is not for sale through any church or by any man. Christ alone controls it. The Holy Spirit applies it. Any sinner anywhere may accept it.

Do make sure, my friend, that you are washed in the blood of the Lamb, so that you may have entrance to the presence of God (Rev. 7:14, 15).